Transforming My Pain

JENNIFER LECLER

Copyright 2021 by Jennifer Lecler

All rights reserved. This book or any portion thereof may not be reproduced or used in any manner whatsoever without the express written permission of the publisher except for the use of brief quotations in a book review.

Limits of Liability and Disclaimer of Warranty

The author and publisher shall not be liable for your misuse of this material. This book is strictly for informational purposes. The purpose of this book is to educate and entertain. The author and publisher do not guarantee anyone following these techniques, suggestions, tips, ideas, or strategies will become successful. The author and publisher shall have neither liability nor responsibility to anyone with respect to any loss or damage caused, or alleged to be caused, directly or indirectly by the information contained in this book.

Unless otherwise indicated, Scripture quotations taken from Holy Bible, New International Version (Copyright (C)1973, 1978, 1984, 2011 by Biblica Inc Used by permission. All rights reserved.

Printed in the United States of America

Jennifer Lecler, Publishing, LLC

www.transformingmypain.com

ISBN Hardcover: 978-1-64184-672-1
ISBN Paperback: 978-1-64184-673-8
ISBN Ebook: 978-1-64184-674-5

Thanks and Acknowledgements

I would like to extend my thanks to the people who have believed in me and have supported me along the way.

Carmen Palomares, our deep friendship, and sisterhood came later in our lives, even though I have known you for most of my life, and now we are thick as thieves!

Rosa Esther Deleon Santiago, I have been forever blessed by your friendship and so glad that God had us meet our first day at college. I thank you for your prophetic utterance regarding this book many years ago and even recently.

P.W., you know who you are, thank you for giving me the name and title of my book. (I know you did not even know that.) As I have told you many times, I thank God for the time that he allowed you and I to speak your support and non-judgmental ways. I will never forget.

To **James McBride**, you were another Godsend in my life the last few years. Your impartial and disarming way of counseling has been what I have needed.

Srey Khmer, I just have no words to express how much your caring heart and love has helped me during this time. You have been my cheerleader in getting my story out. Thank you for your prayers. God bless you always.

Jennifer Carey Reichle, In the midst of all you have been through in the last few years and becoming an author yourself, I thank you for helping me make my 1st book the best it can be. May God continue to bless you and the "boys" Richly.

Crystal Ivette, I am glad to be your God mama. God could not have given me a better person as you are no longer a child, but I am so glad you are in my life and that I get to be in yours.

Cherrybel- We have had so many ups and downs throughout the years; however, you have been happy for me. I pray my story blesses you. You were there as I went through a lot of this.

Lastly, for those who have made fun of me throughout the years, although painful at times, I am glad I have remained my unique self and have never conformed to what people thought or think I should be. I thank you.

The reason for my story.

This all began when at the age of 14 my best friend and I had just come from walking through Central Park. After spending hours together, she came home with me, and we got on the subject of what "our situation" (our life circumstances) was doing to us, and what we were going to do when we got older, I came out of nowhere and said, "when I get older, I am going to write about what has happened to me and people are gonna read it." My friend looked at me like, "ok um… that's good!" What was she going to say to that, but to respond with what she was gonna do when she got older. Once I spoke those words out of my mouth, I was determined. That is exactly what I was going to do.

    Fast forward many years later, I was reminded from time to time of those words, "I am gonna write a book…" I did not take to writing until I was in my late 20's. Then I picked it up again on a chance encounter in 2015 which led me to a published author who let me know that if God was leading me, then what was there to be afraid of? What is known as "chance encounters," I call "divine appointments."

Beside writing this book so that people would know my story, I am writing it because I want the world to know I am here today and have made it thus far not of my own volition, but through the saving grace and mercy of my Lord and Savior Jesus Christ. As you will learn and hear throughout my story, my God has been there every step of the way for me. As long as it is called today, he will always be my reason to live. I could not, nor would I have made it through the things I have experienced without HIM.

My sincerest hope is that my story will open up your "healing, heart and mind" to the one and only True God and the fact that no matter what you have been through or are going through, HE will be there with you every step of the way leading you, guiding you, in the trenches and heal you as you transform your pain.

Table of Contents

Thanks and Acknowledgements iii

The reason for my story. v

Here is where my journey begins 1

My Beginnings 5

The Church Years 32

The School Years 37

My Loves 63

Coping mechanisms and dealing with trauma 83

Present Day 93

A Word of Encouragement and the Gospel 95

For believers 97

Keep In touch 101

Authors Bio 103

Here is where my journey begins

"Abuelito no me toces, abuelito me tocaste, abuelito me toco". In English, the phrase goes "Grandfather, don't touch me. Grandfather you touched me. Grandfather touched me." I had just woken up from this horrific dream and I was angry.

The dream actually began with me in the middle of what was my room with these huge windows. My bed was in the middle of the room and there was a violent thunderstorm outside. In the dream, I woke up frightened, with my eyes wide open. Then I heard 3 voices say abuelito no me toces, abuelito me tocaste, abuelito me toco. I recognized the 3 voices, and they were me saying this to my grandmother in the next part of the dream. But before that, the voices were me as a child, then about 9 years old and then me at the age of 18. The scene changes and I am in the living room of the apartment folding laundry with my grandmother when I tell her that Abuelo (grandfather) touched me. She reacted just the way she would in real life and was angry at me, and at him I suppose. After that I believe I woke up. When I did, to say all "Hell" broke loose is an understatement.

I woke up with a rage that I had not felt until that night, and I was distraught, I did not know what to make of what I just saw. Before I could even acknowledge that disturbing dream, I yelled at God and told him "if what I just dreamed is true, show me now! I am not kidding Lord, don't play with me." Given the circumstances, yes, I was pretty bold, speaking like that to God, but this was no laughing matter and I needed to know if he had abused me. No sooner than I said, "I ain't playing God," a vision flashed before my eyes. I was running around my grandfather's living room, screaming, and crying, pleading, and begging for him not to chase me or hurt me.

My GOD!!! It was true, all of it, I remembered now. I cannot even write into words how that experience was, having to acknowledge that it was true, the man I loved very much, harmed me in the worst way. It all came flooding back. Before I get into more memories, I must say the rage that came over me, at knowing that I was raped and by whom. was horrifying to say the least. I began to wrestle with God, so to speak, and wanted revenge. I wondered if my grandfather could be prosecuted for what he had done to me and perhaps others. I was not a violent person. I had never really fought anyone, but I remembered that the drug dealers who stood downstairs in front of my building would take my request. That was it, I was going to ask one of the kids I went to elementary school with to take my grandfather's life. He had to pay for what he had done to me. Ugh, all these memories, the insurmountable pain. How does someone you love do that to you? Inflict pain and change you in the worst ways; and bring you to the place that now you want him gone?

I could not believe what I was thinking. Me, a Christian and someone who was not so docile, but nice. Over the next few days and weeks, I barely slept, and nightly would contemplate how I was going to handle what happened to me. As quickly as the thought of having someone take my grandfather's life came, I let it go. Hours later. I knew that it was not going to help. Yet the anger and pain burned so hard that I mulled it over in my head for a while, then dismissed it and asked God to forgive me. Next, I considered prosecution. At some point, I called an attorney to find out if he would go to jail for what he did to me. I was informed that because I was 18 the statute of limitations had passed. He no longer could be prosecuted for his past crime against me. I was so disappointed and relieved at the same time. When I thought of how his daughter would respond and my grandmother, I knew that it would be a long and arduous battle if he was to be put on trial for incest and rape. I had been through enough.... could I even survive it?

Next on my plate was letting my grandmother know what happened to me and who had done it. Perhaps even letting, my other family members know. Telling my grandmother was a gamble. She would probably hit me and blame me, in addition to cursing him out. Somehow, I built up the courage to tell her a few weeks after my dream. Her response was typical and a bit surprising to say the least. She did not blame me for the molestation but blamed me for not telling her sooner. To be honest, I said to her," I did tell you when I was little. Don't you remember?" She began telling me that was untrue. So, I left that alone and she began to curse him, just as I figured she would. My grandmother asked when did this happen, and I let her know that It was at his house. I am not sure If I went into all the details of my dream, but I got lectured about being more honest, and speaking up sooner.

I stopped trusting her when I told her about another incident where an 8th grader to my 4th grade self, grabbed me to kiss me and only God knows what else, taking me to another hallway in the school building. At that time, I cried out for someone to help me and told him "no!!!" as he gripped my arm and tried to pull me to him. I was saved when my grandfather walked in to pick me up at school. He asked me what was going on I explained what the kid was trying to do to me as the kid ran away. When my grandfather dropped me off at home and I told my grandmother what happened to me, she hit me on my leg and said I was lying and if it did happen, I provoked it somehow. Not being believed when you tell a parent or trusted person leaves you with a pain that is indescribable. More on that later.

I felt a great relief in telling my grandmother, having severe anxiety, at how she would react to the news and what would that cost me. Surprisingly enough, she was on my side. She was still not someone I could run to, to tell all my feelings, thoughts, or problems to. But we made some kind of headway at that time and she said if I remember anything else to let her know.

My grandfather used an instrument on me that until this day, when I see it stirs up feelings of pain and panic, most times I can deal with it but while it is in my presence, my body goes tight; a tension that is hard to explain. I have had people unknowingly mention that they would like that instrument, or maybe it would bring me relaxation, and again I would feel panic rise and quickly say no, let us not get that I do not like that instrument.

I also have a memory and it might have been the same time he used that "thing" on me. I had woken up in his bed, undressed and in a lot of pain. When I went to the bathroom, I just remember seeing blood. The memory began to surface of what he had done to me and I began to cry. He came in the bathroom asked me what was wrong. I was too little; I could not express what I was feeling and quickly tried to block the memory of what happened to me out of my mind. I wanted to get dressed and have him take me home. If the abuse ended at 3:59, by 4:01, once it was over It was out of my mind. This is how I coped. I realized after my dream at 18, that I would not had been able to handle knowing what had happened to me at that young age. I would have taken my life.

The abuse began at the age of 4 and with him ended at 8 when I was sitting on his bed watching tv with my back turned to him and he lunged at me from behind and grabbed my breasts. I was fed up, this was not going to happen to me anymore, I was getting older and would fight if I had too. I said no and elbowed him so hard that he fell to the floor. I was scared and felt triumphant all at the same time. He never bothered me again.

My Beginnings

I grew up in Spanish Harlem. "El Barrio." "The projects". I am Puerto Rican, American Indian, and Black (there is also Royal blood in my family as my Great Great grandmother on my mothers' side was an African Princess, married to an English White Nobleman.) On my paternal grandfathers' side, I was told that his mother was a Taino Indian. All this just translates to me as Latina. I grew up with my Spanish side, Today I would be called Afro - Latina, and that is ok with me.

Up until a certain age I was a positive child, saw the glass half-full and always looked on the bright side of things before I ever considered the negative. I would smile all the time, at people and would be sad when I would get a look of disdain on certain people's faces who could not even say a simple hello when spoken to. Quickly forgotten, most times, other times staying with the hurt for a little while. I loved the Sun and warm weather. Over time, after the abuse from my abuelo, I started to become more and more silent. Other abuses also began to keep me quiet.

I had such a vivid imagination and would play and fantasize as all children do.

I know that I lived with my mother and father until I was almost 2 years old. We lived not too far from my abuela's house, in fact about 3 blocks to be exact. My mother and father told me stories as I got older that I slept in a drawer because I was so small. I was born in the 7th month, instead of at 9 months and was about 3 pounds. I believe it was my abuela, who is my father's mother, that told me that I was neglected and sent to the hospital. I was malnourished as a baby, so they had to feed me through a tube near my ankle. I still have the scar on my leg, and when I would accidently get kicked there or I hit myself there, it still hurts.

First Dreams:

As a young child my first dream was to be a ballerina. Yes, I know what little girl does not want to be one? However, I was profoundly serious, I had the desire, passion, and discipline to become one. I was 20 pounds overweight but was working on that, learning to eat healthier and better so that I could be part of the "Royal Ballet" one day or any Ballet company. At my young age, I knew that there were not very many dark-skinned Latinas in the Ballet world, but I was going to be one. I had practiced and practiced and adored shows like "Fame" where I knew it was going to take sweat, pain, and tears at times. It was all I wanted. I even managed to get on pointe. I loved it.

One day my abuela asked me what classes I wanted to take at a local studio not too far from our apartment. I told her I wanted to take Ballet. My grandmother asked me instead if I wanted to take piano. I admit at the time I did, However, I was getting older and needed to get into those Ballet classes, if I was going to be able to professionally compete and audition. Nope, she did not want me to take Ballet and told me to forget about. It was piano or nothing else. She would be the one paying for the classes, so it was her way or the highway. I eventually gave into taking piano and then backed out when it came time to go to classes. The inability to pursue this dream became a point of pain and contention in my young adult years, my anger burned against my abuela for not letting me pursue my dream.

Transforming My Pain

Racism:

My entire life even until today, I have experienced racism for being a dark-skinned Latina. I was either praised for being a Black Hispanic that could speak Spanish and had "nice hair" or criticized for being too dark. I have been called a "monkey," "burnt toast," " Black hole," and a few other names. These days, racism revolves around my hair. I have Spanish women of different Latin countries other than Puerto Rico, assuming that my hair is fake, that I put in weaves and hair pieces. Now, I am not knocking anyone who does: I just never have. My hair is all mine.

When it gets blown out, which I have my hair stylist do a lot, my hair gets pretty straight. However, I have also been stared at by strangers and asked if they can see my hair because surely it cannot be real. I have been turned down to have my hair done because of the color of my skin and refused a Spanish newspaper because of the color of my skin. I have been asked why I have a white girls name? I have been discriminated against when it came to certain jobs and passed over to rent an apartment that I so desperately needed during Graduate School because the owner did not want "that Nigger" living in her house.

When I was younger, it hurt so much, and yes, maybe in my world, everyone got along, but that was not the case in real life, certainly not for me. Some have been more polite in at least not coming right out and saying hey you are dark, and you say you speak Spanish, but would instead look at me with disdain. I can recount many times someone would look at me and say. "You? Latina? HA!" and scrunch up their faces as if it were the most disgusting thing, they had ever heard. I wish it were my imagination. It has just happened one time too many. Most hurtful of all is the people I love and trust the most, who are "friends" still being "amazed" that I could be Latina. Anyway, one adapts to the cruelty. I should not have had to, knowing that I still deal with this until today. I suppose I will continue to deal with it until I die. However, it is cool these days to be an Afro- Latina and I am proud to be one.

I can be stubborn about some things. Stubbornness is what kept me from listening at times to the naysayers and the voices that told me I could not do" x,y,z" because of my skin color or race. If you told me that I could not do something I would tenaciously, do it anyway. Racism even plagued me when it came to being told that I could not get into the college I wanted to attend, not to even try. I applied and got into one of the most prestigious colleges, I just chose not to go there.

My Maternal Grandmother:

She was a very pretty lady and had beautiful hair always perfectly curled. I loved her curls. She was a lady. She valued manners and looking good! She practiced what she preached. I know she had a good job and lived in what I called a "fancy building." It had a clean lobby and shiny floors, and an elevator. In my young mind, she must have made lots of money. I definitely wanted a building with an elevator and shiny floors, in a great neighborhood! She was a professional; however, I do not remember what she did. I think it was social work. I was also impressed with her apartment which was carpeted and had huge closets with mirrors on the wall. Super fancy!

The few times I visited her, she was always telling my sister and I to sit up. Proper ladies had good posture, and we were not going to be sloppy children. When it came time to bathe, we had to scrub our knees with Ajax. That was another thing. We were not going to have dark knees. My sister's knees were perfect, mine were dark. It was something that made me feel inadequate. My sister also pointed it out to me. I was not a happy camper but by God I was not going to have dark knees. I would scrub away and while I was there it worked.

Listerine, uh! Another memory of my grandmother Frankie, she made sure we acted and looked like little ladies. Bad breath and dark knees would be our downfall, and she just was not going to have it! My sister and I were annoyed, but we did not always mind it. I sort of embraced it after awhile as I was starting to enjoy being trained by "Miss Manners" herself. I think it was because of her influence, I genuinely wanted to attend a charm school and looked into it. Why Not? I was going to be a cool lady, not stuffy but definitely have the best manners of them all.

My grandmother, along with being a lady, was an alcoholic. She would pass out drunk most nights, and I could smell the liquor on her breath and in the air. It was such a contradiction seeing her passed out on the couch or her table, with the nice clothes and perfectly coifed hair. Those things were never out of place, yet there she would be for most of the night, passed out. Occasionally, she would wake up from her state and say something to us, maybe gibberish, or yell at us for not being in bed. My sister and I at times made fun of her. One night we broke into hysterical laughter because my grandmother, passed out at the kitchen table, had one slipper on and the other slipper coming off the other foot. As we waited for the hanging slipper to drop; once it did, we laughed so hard, we did not know what to do with ourselves. We almost woke her from her slumber and ran out the room to crack up. That was one for the history books according to us kids, my sister and I remembered that day for years after.

Kill that Baby:

My maternal and paternal grandmother were not exactly friends, but they spoke often when my maternal grandma was upset with her daughter and vice versa when My father's mom (abuela) was mad at him. My mom's mom did not want them to be together anymore and come to find out she wanted me to be aborted. Yes, she wrote to my Abuela and told her that she wanted my mom to "kill that baby." My Abuela let me know that this is how my grandmother felt about me when she wanted to tell me that my mom was no good and that is why she left me. I would cry and was traumatized for a long time after reading that note. Why would my abuela keep that note, why would she tell me about it? That was pretty cruel. I was a child. Crushed is what I felt.

I was not particularly close to my grandmother and maybe I had seen her no more than 7 times my entire life and spent a weekend or 2 at her "fancy place". One particular weekend, I do not recall how I wound up at my grandmother's house this one time. I think it was an impromptu, "wanna come visit and see your sister and grandmother this weekend?", I remember saying "ugh, no grandma," but yes to my sister. I was about 11 and really did not want to scrub my knees or sit straight, you, know? pre-teens! Nevertheless, I was happy to see my sister.

I was dropped off at my grandmothers to spend the first night at her house and then spend the next night with my sister and my mom, then go home Sunday evening. Since saying yes, I had an odd feeling in my soul. Something within me changed and I almost spoke up to say, "you know what? Let me come up another day." But I was young and did not want my mom to be disappointed or angry with me. This was rare, a chance to be with my big sis and see my mother for that matter. So off I went in the cab, On the way, my excitement became greater than that voice that kept telling me do not go.

When I arrived at grandmother's, my sister and I smiled and quickly went to her room to play. At some point, the odd feeling returned, and I began to stiffen up. My sister noticed and asked if I was, ok? I began to tell her what I could; however, I could not put my finger on it, I did not feel right, and my sister became concerned.

I remember my grandmother's boyfriend came into my sisters' room to say, "hi" to us. I got chills and this is when my sister turned serious. I remember thinking I want to go home. I should go home!!! Fear filled me, and I did not know why! My spirit knew. A little while later, my sister and I were back to playing and talking. Her mood had lightened, and we were having tons of fun when my grandmother's boyfriend burst into my sisters' room and came after us. He began pawing at us and wanted to rape my sister. We instantly began crying and screaming! We leapt off our beds as he came after my sister. At first, I did not know what to do but tried to get him off my sister. This is when he came onto me and tried to pull my pants down, my sister grabbed a hanger and hit him with it, but he was too strong for her, for us! I honestly do not know what happened after that, because some of my memories are gone or locked away but I wondered where my grandmother was and why was she not helping us as her man tried to rape us. He also spoke some horrible things to us as he attacked us, I thank God he was not able to actually rape us, because my grandmother finally appeared and told him to get away from us, and to leave for the night! Leave for the night????

We were traumatized, almost raped, physically assaulted and she told him to leave for the night! There was no way I could stay there, yet I was torn because I wanted to be with my sister, what would happen to her? I believe we called my mom, and I asked her to come get me. While I waited for my mom to pick me up, I do not remember anything else except that he did not leave right away. He was ranting and raving, saying that he was going to do what he wanted to do. Who did we think we were?

My sister and I just sat there in her room, hurt, terrified, and disgusted with our grandmother, especially when I heard that he was back not too long after the attack.

How could she let him back into the house after what he did to us? I felt emotions that I cannot even describe, more like betrayal, and a hurt that is indescribable, soul injuring. I felt completely unprotected.

When I left, I feared for my sister, and to be honest because my sister was traumatized, when he got off of her and attacked me, my sister did nothing, I was secretly mad her, as I grew- up, I realized and understood as an adult that she was deeply traumatized, and she was also a little girl. However, things were never the same with us until our mother's death in 2008.

Sometime in the late 80's or beginning of 90's I got a call from my mother saying my grandmother was dead, she had been burned alive. Someone she knew came into her home and beat her; I am not sure if they stole from her but set her body on fire. I was horrified and my mother was beside herself. I could not reconcile my feelings regarding this terrifying news. Who would do that to her? Why? She had never hurt anyone. It hurt, but I wondered if I should feel that way because I barely had spoken to her throughout the years. I loved her. She was my grandmother, yet my feelings were at odds. I believe until today, the person has never been found. Her murder remains unsolved.

Mama:

My mama was also a pretty woman with freckles. My mom would turn heads from time to time. She had me when she was 19 years old, and my father was 20. She regaled me with stories of how she and my father played hooky and would smoke cigarettes and other things. Her mom and my abuela (fathers' mother) used to get after both of them to stop skipping school, and when my mother was in trouble for hanging out with my dad, they would take the train and just ride until the storm was over.

My mama was another one who I did not see often once she stopped living with my father. My mother was madly in love with my dad, but she had to leave him because of his womanizing ways. She could no longer take it and picked up and left with my sister to her mother's house, my maternal grandmother. Once she left me, I fantasied as a little girl that my mother would come and whisk me away to her house, and I would find her back with my father. I ached and longed for their reunion, and for me to be able to tell them about my day. It was my usual fantasy and prayer at night.

I never understood why she left me with my dad. Did she not love me? I confronted her on this when I became older, and she told me her intentions was always to come and get me, but my abuela blocked it and wound-up getting guardianship over me. I think my father also protested and did not want me to leave my abuela's.

Mama and I did not really forge a real relationship until I was in college at 21. This was the first time in years she had giving me her number so that I could call her. Prior to this, I had not heard or spoken to her for years. She barely called nor came by to see me much. It was odd and very strange to me that a mother would not give her child her number, but hey this was my family. Come to find out my mother would visit a friend of hers who lived a few buildings away from my abuelas house quite often. The knowledge of that hurt me. Again, why was she not interested in seeing her daughter? Why was she not checking up on me? I was going through heck, I digress…

A foiled Kidnapping:

When I was in Pre-school, I was on my way to the bathroom when I saw my mother at the front door. When I saw her, I froze, smiled, and looked around instantly. I always had like 5 thoughts going on at the same time, so when I looked around, I thought what if the principal sees her? Will they take her away? There is my mom, I want to go to her, but she was not supposed to be here. Did she come to take me away, like wonder woman? Meanwhile, my mother was asking me to come to her, quietly. I was so conflicted. What happens if I do? What about the rules? The principal is mean, will she hurt my mommy. Will my mother take me to another location and harm me? I then became scared. (so much trauma brought on that fear).

no sooner had I decided to go to my mother, and the front door, the Principal appeared and asked, "Who is this woman, Jennifer?" I looked at my mother who told me to not say anything, and at the principal when my mouth betrayed me. Honesty won, and I said, "THAT'S my MOMMY and she is trying to KIDNAP me!" My mother's face fell and asked me why I said anything She was disappointed. Oh, no! I hurt my mommy, what now? Quickly the principal moved to the front desk monitor and asked her to call the cops. I panicked, and a teacher came to safely bring me back to my class. All the kids gathered around me to find out what happened, I told them, my mama tried to Kidnap me.

I became a celebrity for the day and milked it a little bit. The children were fascinated and wanted to know all the details. I began to cry at one point as all my emotions and fears came to the surface. I know I felt pride because my mother did come to kidnap me. I know what she did was wrong as she went to great lengths to do this, yet this showed that she loved me, right?

Mama worked at a Taxi company as a dispatcher. She would call me every few months to say that she was going to pick me up. It would be Brown car #... So, I would prepare myself. My abuela would help me pack my bag, and Friday would come. I would sit by the window to watch every brown car pass by, and the cab would never show up. My excitement would turn to deep disappointment, here we go again, my mama leaving me high and dry. This produced an anxiety in me about being abandoned that as I got older, if anyone I was with would separate from me, I would start to hyperventilate and panic. I would then get angry and sulk or go off on the person who, simply just wanted to look at an item a few aisles down or go get something else, somewhere. For years at first, I would keep all these emotions bottled up, I would be depressed for quite some time. This continued well into my 20's. Now as an adult, I may feel a bit of panic want to rise, yet I know how to calm myself now, and I know that I could take care of myself. If I ever were separated from someone for whatever reason, I would know how to get home or get what I need. That little girl did not.

I am not sure how often I heard from her after this…a little during my junior high school years, to which she came to my graduation and took me out to celebrate. That day was a happy day. In high school I barely heard from her; however, one day I went to run an errand and saw her standing near my favorite library. When I noticed her, I smiled, and I got no response. Ok, maybe she did not see me. I smiled again and waved, she ignored me, looking out towards the crowd but not at me. Why? I was crushed once again. I called her weeks later to speak about that incident. My mother stated that she did not say hello to me because she did not want me to know what she was doing.

I did not hear much from her except for an occasional phone call. Once I was in college, it took about 2 years for me to build trust and feel comfortable just shooting the breeze and chatting her up. It was not until I was 23 that I could say we now had a relationship where calling became common place. One great thing about my mama was that she was hysterical. She had "jokes" she and I would crack up on the phone over the silliest things. We would have a lot of fun.

Our relationship was still rocky in the sense that I did not trust her, in spite of her now being in my life and calling me at least once a week. I questioned her and asked why she had not been there for me when I was younger and why she never came to get me. My mama explained that she always wanted me but that my abuela and father would not let her come get me. Well, that news made me upset, and I could understand that it was true that my abuela and dad did not want me to live with my mother. Once this was brought up, and she finally explained how she felt the healing began.

Sometime after the conversation with my mom, one day after classes at college, all of a sudden, I began to cry. My heart hurt and it was not something I conjured up on my own. I felt as if the pain was forced upon me, as if God were saying now, it is time to move past this and forgive your mom and dad for their abandonment. I started praying and began to cry, so much so that I cried for about 6 hours and could not stop. The next day, I cried for about 5 hours straight. When I was done, I never had to look back and be hurt that my mom and dad lived for themselves or be confused anymore about her wanting me. This chapter finally began to close.

To summarize the last few 4 years before my mother's passing, I loved on her and she on me. We were finally close and could safely, without any repercussions, love. In September of 2008, her husband had a heart attack and died. My mother called me beside herself, saying her love left her. My heart broke for her because I know she loved her husband. During his wake, there was no laughter or a smile on my mother's face. Ironically, she looked so beautiful, with her hair pinned up and wearing her black dress, when my mother yelled out, "I am coming to join you, Jimmy!!!"

A month later, she called me to say she was in the hospital and did not want to leave. My mom did leave the hospital but about a week later she was back in and 3 months later she died. It was 3 days before Christmas. She kept her promise to meet her husband. I learned that one can die of a broken heart. She did. I miss my mama.

My Sister:

I introduced such an incredibly sensitive topic. An attempted rape that happened to us, but I want to say that my sister who is about a year and half older than I, will always be my hero. She has had it tough too. Yet she is still standing. The few times that we got to be together, when we were little, we were called "Irish twins" because we were about the same height and seemed to be the same age for 3 months or so and then she would turn a year older. I remember hearing the term and scrunching up my face because we were not "white" or "Irish", I did not have freckles, but I wanted some. I digress. My sister is and always was very pretty, she was also extremely outgoing and popular among the boys and girls alike. I was the awkward weird little sister and chunky. We loved each other though and of course still do. I admired and disliked at times that she was the one to have all the friends. I was too shy and quiet.

As an adult, when I have seen her, I become that little girl who looked up to her bigger sister. I feel safe with her, as she would mostly protect me against anyone trying to do harm to her little sis. When our mama died, we became close, and my sister handled my mother's affairs like a champ. We remained close for about 4 years after my mothers' death. Since then, we have not seen or been in each other lives except for the occasional phone call.

My Uncle:

Papi, that is what my abuela called him. Well, because she nicknamed him that, we all called him that. Papi was the oldest of my abuela's children. He loved to dress in his best suits and Kangol hats. He was always dressed (curro), basically in Spanish dressed to impress and clean. I know my uncle wanted to be a chef; this was one of his life's ambitions. He loved to cook and was good at it. His other aspiration was to be a Salsero, Papi played the Guido and a few other instruments. He was even on a few Salsa albums; I remember seeing his name on the credits.

I dearly loved Papi. He used to come to visit abuela almost every day. He would help his mom out with whatever she needed. When he came, he would eat and then we would sit in the living room and we would chat about sports, his latest recipe or music. Often times he would ask me how was I doing in school and if I was alright? As I got older, I began to realize that something was not quite right with my uncle. He would tell me that other people were talking about him or that there were rats in the wall, that spoke to him. It was not until one day I learned that he was Schizophrenic, I believe he told me himself.

I had no clue what that meant, I just knew that he was ill. His mental illness derailed him from becoming a chef and salsero. He was so good at both, I wanted him to succeed and hoped that he would just overcome. Once I began to read up on Schizophrenia and its symptoms, I understood that unless he took his medicine, he was not going to be able to accomplish his goals. I still rooted for him for a while.

His schizophrenia began to ruin a lot of our good times and I decided as I got older, I did not want to be around him as much. He would be volatile at times towards his mom and that was always hard to watch. It was difficult and painful being in the midst of this, Not knowing if he would succeed in hurting my abuela, or if he would be hauled away by the police. There were several such incidents, where the police had to be called on him. Then there were 2 major fights I had with my uncle. One was when we were at my abuela's, and he asked me if I wanted a dollar? I said "yes," and believe I grabbed it from him. He laughed at first and so did I. It was a game, right? Well, he turned serious and asked for his dollar back. I teased and said, "No, I am going to keep it!" He then became angry and grabbed my hand with the dollar in it. He grabbed so hard he scratched me and broke skin. I let the dollar go told him what he did, and he became even angrier at me.

I was home alone so, I had to think fast. What was I going to do? As he became more and more angry, I got up and ran to the kitchen to grab a knife to protect myself. I was not into violence, but I was alone, and his anger and strength were no match for me, a teenage girl. He then started murmuring under his breath and threatened me. He had never gone this far and over a dollar? I tried to get him out of the house, but he would not leave. I really began to fear for my life. I began to pray furiously and asked God what to do? When I realized it was Friday, Youth Night! It was early, but maybe I could go and hang out at the church. So, I grabbed my keys and left the apartment. Come to find out my uncle was fast on my heels and found me at church, prior to this when I arrived, miraculously my youth counselor was there, I told her what happened that my uncle threatened my life and so I grabbed a knife out of the kitchen to defend myself. As she was thanking God that I was safe, my uncle came towards us cursing and yelling at me.

At that point, my youth counselor, scared and all, fended him off by telling him to leave me alone or she would call the cops on him. He was not having it. We had to run inside the church and close the gate so he would not continue to come after us. Someone else was inside the church and heard all the commotion and got him to leave. I was distraught and remember blaming myself because I played with him and would not give him his dollar back. I was afraid to go home or walk home by myself because he could be hanging out waiting for me. I also never wanted to see him again, yet that was impossible because he still came to his mom's house. I feared for awhile that he might kill me, and I would be helpless to defend myself.

My best friend at the time was at my house. She was staying with me for a few days, perhaps even a week. At one point we were lying on my bed when she heard a commotion outside. I got a funny feeling and began to hear it too. There was a man outside cursing and throwing a garbage can around. I began to recognize the voice as it came closer to our building. I was frightened because so many shootouts had been happening right outside my window and in the area. Also, violent fights were the norm.

My bestie got up and decided to look out the window. I instantly became upset. She then said, "wait, is that your uncle?" "Oh, my gosh, I am so scared. Is he coming up here?" "He better not!" "Why is he throwing garbage? What is wrong with him?" I was mortified, sad, and wondered what had happened for him to act this way, Papi was in fact on his way up! My Lord, what now? Were we in danger? My friend wanted to leave. There was my uncle at the door. He knocked and my abuela opened the door. She began to cry and asked him what happened to him. My friend said, "do not go out there (to the living room) or he will hurt us." I shut her up and went to see what was wrong with my uncle. His face was badly bruised and bleeding.

My uncle began to recount who hurt him. A world of hurt was heaped upon me. He was my family for Pete's sake! I disliked him, deeply loved him, and felt pity and anger all at the same time. I came to find out that the kids I went to elementary school with had hurt him. They beat him because of his illness. He apparently got snotty with one of them and things turned sour from there. When I confronted them a few days later, they told me that he was lucky that he did not kill him. Man, my heart was crushed and frightened for him.

My uncle did not come around for a few weeks, and we begged him to stay clear of those boys. I was happy not to see him. Then it was time for me to go to college, and I was not going to be around him all the time. Ironically enough, he had written me in college a few times to see how I was doing. It comforted me and frightened me all at the same time. Since he was schizophrenic, one never knew what he was going to write. I certainly did not want to relive the past where "rats", spoke to him through the walls and people overheard our conversations when no one was around. To my surprise his letters were always pleasant and short.

He truly just wanted to know how I was and to let me know that he missed me. Those letters comforted me because he still cared.

Advancing to my last year in college. I got a call from my grandmother, she explained that his cancer had progressed, and was in the hospital. I had to see him. We did not know how long we had with him. I came home that particular weekend from college. My bestie wanted to hang out and I told her that I needed to visit my uncle in the hospital as we do not know how long he has to live. My bestie asked me if I wanted her to accompany me, I said her "yes, please." When we arrived at the hospital, I took a moment to ask God to forgive me for the hate I felt towards my uncle, and for how mean I had been to him the last few years of his life. I did not want to live with regrets. I then asked my friend if I could see him alone. She understood. I walked into his hospital room, he saw me and turned his head towards me. He was hooked up to so many cords and things, I just began crying, I asked him how he was feeling, and he could not even speak. He just shook his head as to say, "I am ok." He really was not.

I then said between sobs, "Papi, I love you and I am sorry for the way I treated you the last few years." I asked him if he would forgive me? He began to shed a few tears and in a very soft voice he said, "I forgive you!" I bursted into more tears. He also asked me to forgive him, and I said, "do not worry about that, there is nothing to forgive". I held his hand and then said my goodbyes. He was getting tired, and I could see the strain in his eyes. It was hard for him to speak so I left. Once I got into the hallway, my friend held me, as I cried in her arms. When I composed myself, we left. I never saw my uncle again. I was in Europe performing when I got the call that my uncle passed away on August 10th, 1996. Rest in Peace, Papi.

Uncle Junior:

My abuela's middle son. Tall at 6'3 and handsome like the rest. I had a pretty interesting relationship with him. He liked to tease me, that would stay with him until his death in 2019. When I was a baby, he would say that Cuco (monster) was going to get me, I would look in the direction of the closet he would point to, and just wail. My mother would come in and reprimand him. He would just laugh. He had a hardy laughter. He was the fun uncle, and sometimes I would go and visit him at his house when he lived in the Bronx. He used to come visit him mom and stay to eat as most Hispanics do. You cannot come to abuela's house and not eat. My abuela was one of the best cooks around. Rest in Peace Junior. Jan 26, 2019

My two Cousins:

These two, a girl and a boy came to live with my abuela at 2 months and 5 months, respectively. What a joy! The girl named Lorraine came into our family when I left for Nyack college. Christian came a year later. Those two were like twins, not just because they were close in age but rather because they loved each other, were one another's sounding board and hung out with one another daily. They also held competitions about who would do better in school. They are and were extremely intelligent and soared in school. Lorraine is now a grown woman, working hard and living life. Christian on the other hand was taken from us way too soon. He was killed in Jan 2015. He was working on his master's degree before this tragic event. He brought so much joy to many and was a mentor to many as well. His death has left a mark on me, and even though I think about him often, I do not speak much about him because after a while I just can't hold back the emotions associated with his loss. Love you much, Christian! Jan 6th, 2015.

My Dad:

My Father was 6'1, lanky and skinny as heck. Even when he gained a little weight, he was still a bean pole. He was the baby of the family, among 2 older brothers. The baby had a baby at

20, and that was me. As I noted in the beginning, my father and mother lived together just 3 blocks or so from my abuela. He would drop me off, at my grandmother's house and would pick me up to go to our apartment. I remember that a few times.

In my eyes, no one could hold a candle to my father. He was so handsome and fun. So much so that when he occasionally came to visit me at school, the girls in my class would giggle and get all googley eyed, then ask me "who is that, Jennifer? Is that your DAD?" They would get the cheesiest grins, and with my head held high, would proudly say, "yes, that is my DAD!!!" "Oooh, he is sooooooo handsome," they would squeal. Internally, I would say to myself, "I know" and then get jealous, like he is my daddy, stop looking at him.

After my dad went off to make his life, he settled in what us New Yorker's call "upstate" Come to find out it was Westchester County! Nevertheless, He had a job as a social worker and owned a condo not too far from his Job. I did not see my father often much like my mom, but I visited him and even lived with him for 6 months. I was about 6 years old

During those 6 months, I fell in love with Upstate and wanted to live there forever. There were woods behind his home, I would go there and sing and pray to God. I loved it. The love boat was popular at that time so I would swing off of a tree and sing the theme song of the "Love Boat" I also enjoyed the friends and "boys" I met while there. I had lots of fun.

The women in My Dad's Life:

I mentioned that my daddy was handsome and all. Many women loved him. He loved the ladies just as much, so much so that he was a " womanizer." There were many women who came and went and some that stayed for a while longer. One of those women was his first wife. Her name was "Mami Ellie" Mami Ellie was a pretty dark-skinned Puerto Rican lady, from Puerto Rico. I know my dad told me how they met, but I do not really remember well. The few times I would visit my dad in his Westchester condo, she was nice to me and kind. She took care of me well and cooked so good. However, their arguments overtime became more frequent, and she took them out on me, and I began to dislike her. She hit me a few times, and my dad would hit her for hitting me. There were 2 other incidents that made me never want to see her again. Besides the (fuetes), she would give me (spankings and slaps).

I was playing around with a doll that she had given me, it was a Raggedy Ann doll, that was my height. One could slip their feet into hers and dance around with her. That is what I loved to do. So, as I danced around with Raggedy Ann, Mami Ellie had gotten into a fight with my father and she came storming into the living room and slaps me in the face, then proceeds to take my doll from me. I was stunned, hurt and angry. I did not do anything to her, why would she hit me? This woman did not hit lightly either. I was sad for a good while, until she gave me my doll back. I also tried to stay away from her as best as I could during my visit. I remember her holding me at one point and saying she was sorry while she cried. I had mixed emotions. But I forgave.

The last incident I had with Mami Elie was during lunch at my father's house. She had given me a can of cheese raviolis. I knew I did not like them from the moment she opened the can. I asked her to please not give that to me or I was going to throw up. I was not being willful or defiant, it was just, the smell, the look of it, grossed me out. Well, she was the type of person, who like most parents or caregivers growing up that would say, "you are going to eat what I put in front of you!" Or you risked being spanked. In my case, punched, smacked ridiculously hard across the back or face, and hair pulling was what happened. Well, I began to eat it. I had no choice. No sooner did I start eating, When, I explained to her that It was making me sick," please do not have me continue to eat it." She yelled I ate, then came the upchuck. I threw up in my raviolis. Mami Ellie yelled, slapped me across the back and then said she was going to tell my abuela what I did. She then made me eat some more raviolis now with the throw up in it. I was so mad, I told her I did not care if she hit me again. Her rage grew and I am not sure if I was punished because of it. Mami Ellie packed up the raviolis and off we went back to my abuelas house. When we arrived, she quickly told her what I had done. that I purposely threw up in my food.

She thought she had my abuela in her pocket when Mami Elie explained that I was impolite and talked back to her. She then showed her the ravioli with my throw up in it. I spoke out and said she made me eat it with the throw-up inside. My abuela said "what?" and proceeded to put Mami Ellie in her place. I had never been happier. For once my abuela stood up for me instead of siding with the adult. My abuela told her to never, ever give me throwed - up food again or she would deal with her instead. Shortly after that, she was fed up with my dad and left him and moved back to Puerto Rico. After her treatment of me I said, "good riddance."

The next significant woman in my dad's life was a woman whom I grew to love as a mother. She was a Caucasian woman and had the bluest eyes and blondest hair. I remember meeting her for the first time. I was so upset at first because again, he was my daddy, and I did not want to share him with anyone. I barely saw him as it is. Plus, I was upset with my father because he would use me as his bait to lure women, without me knowing it. I was still incredibly young, still about 6, and I began to feel uncomfortable going with him to "pick-up" things, as it always involved some woman. They would try to speak to me, and I did not like it. Some looked shady to me. Anyhow, he asked me if I wanted to meet his new lady, and by the sound of his voice, I knew she was special. The woman got out of the car and was really pretty and sweet. However, I went to meet her and was mean to her and wanted nothing to do with her. I could tell she was sad by my response.

Over time, I let down my guard toward her and fell in love with G. I will name her that to protect her identity. G was always kind to me, never yelled and let me comb and brush her hair. I loved to brush her hair. She was my living Barbie. G made sure I went to do fun activities, such as the Brownies and going on excursions to The Land of Make Believe. Towards the end of her relationship with my dad. G had showed me some beautiful Indian earrings, that I thought were so pretty, colorful, and exotic. I asked her if I could put them on? G explained that they were incredibly special to her and that I was not to touch them without her.

One night G was getting ready for a date with my dad when I asked her once again, "may I please see your earnings? G conceded and said "please, please, take care of them". I was so happy she was going to let me try on her earrings, I promised her I would put them back safely in her box when I was done.

I did just that while they were on their date. All was well. Not too long after that, I was confronted with had I taken her earrings? I told her "no, I had not." She said I was the last one to have them. I then explained that I put them in the box. My father came into the room and acted as If I stole her earrings, and I wondered why he was saying that. After G asked me over and over, if I took her earrings, crying, she left the condo and told me she was disappointed in me and could not trust me anymore. Once she was gone my father let me know that he took the earrings and buried them outside the window. I asked him why he would do that, he knew that G would be upset. Why blame me??? My father did not answer my questions but wanted me to keep his secret.

The last significant woman in his life was my brother's mom. He seemed to last with her the longest until one day she took my baby brother back to their home in Connecticut. My father did not get to see his son, my brother, except one or two times after she left. He died without getting to see him, which was one of his greatest desires. My Bothers, mom left because of my dad's abusive ways and also because of his womanizing. All 3 women, I found out at one time or another, left him because of that, among many other terrible things, I found out about my father.

In my mind, the time I spent with my daddy was always a great time; however, I had a secret. My dad and I would play a game that no one should play with her father. My dad was one of my molesters. In my young mind, I was ok with it because I loved him, and he loved me. In truth, I was manipulated and later realized just how traumatized I was. I know other things happened to me, but I cannot remember what, even now I have no clue. I just remember being sent outside after "whatever happened' to play. The memory has never come back to me. I think the Lord knew I would not be able to handle it.

Abuelo:

My paternal grandfather was also a good-looking man with hazel eyes. He was also hard of hearing. My abuelo lived on the other side of our "projects" all one had to do was cut through my building and cross the street, walk past 3 or 4 buildings and one was right there. My grandfather worked in a candy store, and I was the benefactress of bags of penny candy and even 5 cent ones, quite often. I even got to play store and serve up candy in the little brown paper bags. When people wanted 50 cents worth of candy, I would have a little trouble counting but always did ok in the end. My abuelo would pick me up from school and we would either pasear (walk about town) or go to his home.

With him is where my story started, I was 18 years old when I had that vision that cold January morning. The abuse started at the age of 4 and ended at the age of 8, when he came up behind me while I was watching television at his house and lunged at me, grabbing my breasts. I got so angry and frightened that I elbowed him so hard that he fell to the ground. I shouted "NO!" and gave him a "do not mess with me look." He was stunned, but I could not endure it anymore.

He stopped touching me and hurting me; however, up until the age of 15 when he would see me with my friends, he would look at me lustfully the way a man looks at a woman when he wants her. He would do cat calls at me along with his old man friends. They would all say how beautiful I was and how well developed I was. I was thoroughly disgusted. One particular day, I was walking with one of my girlfriends from school, and

I refused to look at him except to say a quick hello. That friend bursted out loudly and said," "Ewww, is that your grandfather, Jennifer?" " Why is he looking at you like that?" Talk about being mortified! I was humiliated and wanted to hide. Instead, I got angry with my friend and told her she was wrong and pushed her away from my abuelo and his friends so that we could go home. That friend would not let it go. I told her she was crazy and Imagining things because it was the truth and she noticed. I continued to try and change the subject to no avail.

Another time, my school friends and I had a long lunch, and I was near the playground where my abuelo lived. When he saw me, he invited me upstairs to eat and drink orange juice which was apparently my favorites at the time; still is actually. I wanted to drink my juice but did not want to leave my friends. I invited them to come for some juice too. Some were unsure, and I remember thinking I was not too sure about this either. I had all these repressed memories, but my body knew something was not right. They followed me to the elevator, and we all went up to his floor.

We all sat down on his couch and chair, waiting for that oj. No sooner does my grandfather serve us girls, he began to growl and laugh hysterically. I panicked and, in my heart, said "NO, not again!", I begged my grandfather to leave my friends alone. I had to hit my grandfather to get him away from my friends. One of them began to cry and said she had to go. The other 2 followed her and ran out the door. I called after them, praying that they would still be my friends after this and worst of all not tell our teacher what just happened because I would then go to jail. These were my thoughts. I went back to class, shaken, broken and afraid to speak to anyone, much less the girls. They eventually and slowly began to speak to me and told me they loved me, but they would never ever be around my grandfather again. I thanked God that they still would be my friends. I did not deserve it after what he tried to do. That is how I felt, anyway, because I blamed myself for his abuse.

In junior high school, I had a few instances where I would be making out with a boy and at some point, I would black out. There would be these black images of two figures in a struggle, one older and one younger running around an object. I would also feel panic and anxiety and hear screaming coming from the smaller figure. Come to find out the image was me running around my grandfather's living room with him in pursuit, chasing me and my screaming for him to stop. I was so little and beyond terrified. When the Lord revealed to me that my grandfather was one of my abusers through the dream, that image finally came into focus.

My Paternal GrandMother (abuela):

I began to live with my abuela when my dad dropped me off at her apartment because he had to work. He seemed to never come back, except occasionally. I know that was not totally true as I mentioned that I visited him at his upstate condo. For a couple of years, it was every summer and then I got to live with him for 6 months during my 6th year. Prior to this, I kept hoping my dad would come get me. My abuela was not a nice woman. She was pretty stern and yelled a lot.

After not being with my dad or my mom, being abandoned by both, my abuela would play this cruel game with me where she pretended, she was going out to throw the garbage out or just pretend that she left. I would hear the door and wait for her to come back in. For what seemed like an eternity, she would not come back inside the apartment. I would go to the door to listen for her thinking maybe she could not get the garbage down the chute, but I was too little to open the door and help her. I would then begin wailing, fearing something happened to her, feeling frightened because she left me too. I would be beside myself, when she would come in and laugh at me, "saying what is the matter? Or worse," what are you crying about? I did not leave you." I would be inconsolable for a while. How could she do that to me? Laugh at me and tell me I was stupid for crying?

It got to the point where I would have to pretend that it did not bother me, or she would berate me for it and even get angry with me. It was neither funny nor ok, but I had to pretend it was so she would not criticize me further. She got a good kick out treating me this way.

From the ages of 4-10 my grandmother physically abused me. I was hand slapped (mano plaso) and given pow pow (a spanking) but the serious abuse was when she would grab me and begin punching me in my back, so hard that my lungs would come forward to my chest and I could not breathe. She would pull my hair and try to choke me. I hated her for this…what did I do to deserve this? Beating me in my back happened at least 4 other times. The last time I remember thinking please "God get her off me, or I will hurt her, I cannot breathe." I wept as I thought like that, but I had to make her stop somehow. I felt like the most wicked sinful person there was. I begged and cried for her to stop hitting me. I would tell her that "I could not breathe" she would laugh! Told me I was stupid and other things I cannot mention, she would curse at me and tell me I deserved this for being mouthy and just being me.

I do not think I could forgive her for a long time… but thankfully it was the last time she hit me that way. I think that she knew that it would get ugly, because as she was constantly hitting me, she antagonized me and would say "WHAT, YOU WANT TO HIT ME?!?!" I DARE YOU!!! She would spew out more hurtful words and then would just leave the room.

On a particular Sunday, my abuela had been upset and angry all day. I was not sure why. When we came back home from church, it was evening around 6 or 7pm. 2 of my favorite musical shows was on. Barbara Mandrel and the Mandrel Sisters, and Donnie and Marie. I went to go turn on my television in my room when my grandmother told me not to. Being the stubborn girl that I was went to turn on the TV anyway. That angered her even more. I finally asked her why I could not watch TV? I always watched these shows. She refused to answer me. I knew it was because she was mad about something that day. I decided to defy her, I could not give up watching my shows, and turned on the tv low, hoping she would not hear it. Of course, she did, and came into my room and said if I do not turn that tv off she was going to "break my neck!"

I was terrified yet thought she would not do that to a little kid, I am her grandchild, whatever…. I lied down, horizontally on the bed and began enjoying the music when my abuela came into the room and tried to make good on her promise. She grabbed me by the neck and tried to twist it and break it, I was horrified, scared and angry at the same time… I quickly prayed that she would not succeed. As she was pulled on my neck, she hurt me. At some point, I was able to turn in such a way that I got away from her grip on my neck. I believe she turned off my tv at that point and huffed away to her room shutting her door, and then giving me the silent treatment for days. I sat on my bed in stunned silence.

During a particularly contentious week with my grandmother, I was tired of the yelling and physical and verbal abuse. At the age of 8, I began planning to run away from home. What a scary thought. On the news were stories of what happened to runaways, I did not want to suffer a similar fate. I remembered from commercials and the News program 20/20 that there was a number you could call. Children were removed from their homes and placed with a loving family. That is what I wanted, to be taken to a better place, so that I did not have to live with my abuela anymore. Any place would be better than here, with her. I did not know how to really use the yellow pages, but I figured it out and stumbled upon ACS. Once I did, I became really scared. Here was my lifeline, maybe? Yet I could not bring myself to call at that moment. I also was nervous and scared that my abuela would find out and do worse to me than anything she had ever done. I bookmarked the page to come back to it someday. I put the yellow pages back where I got it from and tried to calm my fast heartbeat. Silently, I continued to pray throughout that day that my abuela would not find out what I had done.

A few days later, while my abuela and I were sitting in the living room, she just decided to mention that "I wasn't slick, Am I crazy?" I had no clue what she was speaking about. She continued, "What was I thinking, did I want her to get in trouble?" When she then pulls out the yellow pages from the desk it was in and shows me the page, I booked marked. I said nothing as she asked me, "Why?" I felt betrayed and upset with God, I had asked him to protect me from her finding out that I wanted to leave. My abuela let me know that if I ever did something like that again, there would be "hell" to pay.

Now older, Abuela and I were arguing, I am not sure about what, but it did not matter because this was typical. However, I must have answered her back when she asked me a question yet, she did not like me answering her, but she kept asking me to and in my confusion, I got angry and looked at her when she lunges at me and tells me that she will break my lips in Spanish! I was in the hallway of our apartment when I thought "oh, no! not again" and tried to run towards the front door to escape. She reached me and grabbed my lips. I actually paused for a second because I was in complete disbelief that she would harm me this way. Well, she went for it and almost succeed in separating the part of the lip that connects to the bottom of my gums. By the grace of God, he allowed her to get her grip off my mouth before she could finish her mission.

The Church Years

At the age of 4, I started attending church with my abuela. Not by choice but because I had too. I did not mind. I loved my church and enjoyed the choir, which my abuela was a part of. I believe I had even seen my abuela baptized. One of the best days of my life when one of my Sunday school teachers at the time introduced me to Jesus. She had explained that there was this man who came to earth then died for my sins. She also let us kids know that he loved us. Wait, what, someone loved me? He loved me so much that he was hurt for me. I ate that up like a sponge. I am actually loved. I really did not feel that I was until my teacher told me about Jesus. From then on, I accepted him into my heart and strived to live for him as best as a 4-year-old could. Until 8 years old when I decided church was boring. I also wanted to curse. Yup, me as an 8-year-old, I liked being spicy. In my backslidden state, I was struggling so much not to give in to temptation and do what everyone else was doing. So, I returned to the Lord for good at the age of 15 when during a volleyball game at school, I had heard the Lord ask me to choose HIM or the World. I stopped and contemplated what He asked of me, then answered, "I choose you Lord!"

My first Pastor's name was Reverendo Santiago, he was in his 70's. I adored Rev. Santiago, His sermons used to make me cry every Sunday. His preaching was so simple, yet it reached your heart. He also was very understanding and down to earth. His disposition was usually very jovial. One day he was preaching at the pulpit when he collapsed and fell to the ground. The entire congregation gasped and began to cry. I cried seeing him collapse not knowing if he had passed on.

Someone called 911 and when the ambulance came, they let us know that he was still breathing but was not conscious. He was taken away and as a church we prayed for him and cried together. No one knew what to do, and neither did we want to leave the church. After a while, we did and waited to hear about his progress. If I am not mistaken. Rev. Santiago died a few weeks to months later. We were as a congregation, heartbroken. A great man had gone to be with the Lord. Who would lead us now? After his passing, the church became divided and became a place of much discord, with who was in charge now and who do we hire next and other political divides.

I loved my church that I had attended since I was 4 and left when I was 24. When I became a part of the youth, I started to feel wanted and welcomed. I was a part of something. I had good wholesome friends, whom my grandmother could trust. Although she was still possessive over me and trusted no one. I used to go out to eat with them on Sundays when I could. I have wonderful memories, times of Bible study and meeting at one of our youth counselor's house to fellowship, eat, and be free from the stuffy rules of the church. McDonalds was another place to hang or go to eat or bring back to the church before service began again. Good times. I am thankful for my experiences at my first church.

There were several bad experiences that I had within the church that shaped my life. Some of my early memories were of being mistreated and lied about because for some reason, the leaders did not want me to be a part of Children's church. I was young, so I am not sure why that was so. Like many other experiences, it could have been because of my skin color. Why they started out rejecting me is beyond me.

Subsequently, my abuela celebrated my birthday with the children. The superintendent at the time, only gave me one piece of my birthday cake and when I asked for another slice, she got angry, called me greedy and said there was no more.

The service had ended and my abuela came down to pick me up and I could see her smiling, but she saw my face, and asked me what was wrong. I told her that my teacher would not give me my cake and was mean to me. My abuela, went "buck wild;" in the church and told her off! Yet another, time, this person lied to my grandmother and told her that I did something that I did not do. My abuela knew I would not and never had done what this woman accused me of. She caught her in the lie, and put her once again in her place, but to my dismay, the superintendent, gave me dirty looks for weeks and would not speak to me or call my name at all when I asked questions.

When I discovered that I could sing, the teachers chose the usual suspects to sing in the upcoming cantata. I got a bout of courage and raised my hand when they asked, "who would like to sing?" My hand was ignored by the cake stealing lady and said, "I choose, so and so!" I became sad. One of my other teachers stood up for me and stated that "Jennifer said she would like the part. Let's give her a chance!" Reluctantly, she said, fine, Jennifer can sing the soprano part". She was not happy, and I was nervous by her reaction. I could not understand why she did not like me. I was once again treated with disdain for a time after that. Needless, to say the cantata came and went. I sang, I was proud of myself for singing, and the church people had good things to say.

Burnt toast:

In the children's department there were all age ranges. There were older children who were intimidating and very much treated us little ones like peons. I was 6 years old and there was one girl in particular who I looked up to and tried to be friendly with. She was funny, and I understood her sense of humor. She happened to be standing by the water fountain with 3 other girls when I approached and smiled at her, drank some water, and smiled back at her again. It was then that she snickered at me and asked why I was so dark? I looked like burnt toast. I became crestfallen and also afraid of her after she called me that. I admired this much older woman (in my 6-year-old eyes), I was embarrassed and hurt. I carried her "slur" towards me for an exceedingly long time and any time I saw her, I would run in the other direction. I was afraid that she would hurt me.

That 'older woman' who turned out to be only 3 years older; she and I became friends in our teenage years. From time to time, I would remember what she had said to me but did not dare bring it up. Fast forward 30 years later, and I let her know that her comment was very hurtful to me. She deeply apologized and confessed that she was a hurt kid who hurt others. Turns out she was jealous of my skin color and wished that she had my darker hued complexion. All the while, most of my life, I wished I had her 'light and sweet' coffee colored skin. Now we are thick as thieves; all has been forgiven and forgotten.

Inappropriate Moments:

As I got older, I had moments where I was hit on by a few of the men in the church. One of them happened to be my best friend's father. He had asked me to go to a hotel with him, yes, right in the church! This man was married, I said no, that was not appropriate and wondered how I was going to reveal this to my friend? If I did, she would get angry with me and not be friends anymore. Her mother disliked me for no apparent reason and at times would tell her daughter that she did not want me to hang around her. Once I rebuffed her father, her mother began to like me, and he started telling his daughter not to hang around me. It was a weird situation.

Many men in the church would give me inappropriate stares and "compliments" about my body or how good I looked that day. Moments like that were extremely hard and frightening at times. Most of the time I was angry. How could these men, who were supposed to be saved, sanctified and some married, do this to a teenager and then young adult.

Not all my experiences were bad. When I decided that I was going to take my relationship with God seriously, the trials got harder, yet I grew in HIM and so did my responsibilities. At the age of 16, I debuted as a soloist. Between the ages of 16-21, I became a choir member, co-director of the youth choir, treasurer of the church, treasurer of the youth, and Vice President of the youth. My other responsibilities in church included from time to time leading the church on a Sunday morning in song and Bible Verse (or as we called it Devocionales) Devotionals. I also lead prayer meetings in Spanish and Bible studies on Youth night.

As proud as I was that God had entrusted me with all of these jobs, and I loved each one, when I had them, I became burnt out. I wanted to be perfect in everything, and everyone expected that of me. It became too much. I was at a place that I was expected to never say, "no" to anything. Well, the day came, and I screamed at one of the leaders after I wanted to take a small break and go eat lunch. He wanted me to do something that was not even a part of my position, I yelled and told him, "NO! I want to go eat lunch." I would like to say I was able to just go, and everything was perfect, but instead, I got guilt-tripped and heard "the how can you say no?" You call yourself a Christian?" "It is your duty!" In the past, during the early years I would have given in. Well not that day! I stood up for myself, went to lunch, digested my food, and then went on about my duties and my business.

The School Years

Elementary Years:

I was a fairly quiet kid in school except when it came to my best friend or anyone else in my circle of friends. My grandfather used to call me Cotora (parrot) because I would speak so much. Until I stopped speaking (trauma induced). I was bullied a lot for the way I was dressed and also for being quiet. For some reason, the girls in my class would want to beat me up. At one point, I was so scared to go to school as the bullies' threats were becoming more and more prominent and suggestive at what they were going to do to me. I was followed home from time to time, all the while praying that these girls would not harm me. If and when I shared this with my grandmother, she would tell me how to fight and not allow anyone to hit me. I was still frightened and did not want to fight. My father would say the same, not to let anyone hit me.

As I hit Junior High school, I was a bit bolder and was ready to fight if I had to. Back in the day, we were taught to take off our earrings and put Vaseline on our faces so if someone tried to scratch you, their fingers would slip off your face. I will never forget getting my hair braided and having a crowd of my friends cheering me on. The person did not show up. So, I won the fight by default. I am not going to lie. I was glad not to have to fight.

Being voluptuous at a young age was hard on me. Most of the boys in my class just wanted to touch me. They would attempt to all the time. I hated being touched without my consent. I did not know how to defend myself or stop them since they would touch me and run. It made me feel awful and made me despise having hips and a bust at such a young age. Sometimes it really was devastating because it reminded me of the sexual abuses I had suffered at the hands of family members and friends of the family.

I was abused by more people than I can count on 2 hands, the majority family. I suppose the boys thought I was "loose" because of it; however, I was not, and would yell at them to stop, swat at them, or hit them. Most of the time I did not tell anyone not even my teachers. I would just suffer in silence. It did not help that one day my father was standing outside of my classroom looking into the window and witnessed a boy touch me and run. He walked into the classroom and spoke with the teacher, but when he came to my seat, he was burning with anger and actually called me a "sl*t!!!" I was hurt and crushed in my spirit for a long time.

During my elementary years, my best friend was the one I hung out with the most. We would spend our days and evenings together. I would go to her house or she would come over to mine, and when I was allowed to speak on the phone, after spending 8 or more hours with her, we would gab some more. We even used to laugh about spending all that time together, having so much to say to one another on the phone. I suppose this is normal during the childhood years. I came to find out my best friend was jealous of me. That is not something I ever wanted to believe about anyone concerning me. However, she came out and admitted to me that it was true. I confronted her about some comments said about me. I was told that she cursed me behind my back, said that all I did was complain about my abuela and was a "B." When she told me that was true, she did say those things, I severed my years - long friendship with her.

My bestie tried to come back into my good graces over and over and over again, yet I was done with her betrayal. I was saddened by this loss, but there comes a time when after you have forgiven, you have to move on. So, I did.

She is going to be a star:

One of my father's girlfriends had called my grandmother to see how I was doing and to speak to her about my father. At one point, I heard her say that I was going to be star, that I had a lot of talent. My abuela responded, "no, she is not. She is not going to be a star "she is…. "hearing that crushed me. I was dumbfounded. How could she say something like that? My father's girlfriend knew that I acted and had done a play at school where I was all the rage. Weeks after it, I had teachers tell me that I was headed for stardom; however, my grandmother said I was not. I can tell you that it affected me so much. I would not sing act or dream about my goals for a long time as a result.

I had choreographed a dance, a "salsa" in my class that was performed to good review; This was another moment that my classmates and school let me know that I had talent and was going to be somebody. Yet, every time I went home, I was cast down and told I was being to this or that and as a result, I had begun the pattern in my life where I did not take opportunities to sing, act, dance or write. I would get the courage and then be pushed down with much criticism and harsh words.

At this young elementary age, I loved school and education. I loved learning new words and speaking well. In my home, I was told that I was "white" or trying to be. My abuela would get mad sometimes when I used a word that she did not understand so instead of just asking me, she would tell me I am trying to be a "white person" and "Who did I think I was?"

Junior High School:

We called ourselves the "Diamond Girls" we were a group of 5 and we wore turquoise and pink every Tuesday. The boys in our "crew" had a name as well. We modeled ourselves after a song by T.K.A. called "Diamond girls". We were "fly" lol. Yes, I still use some words from the 80's. That is just me. My "crew" and I were a tightknit group who looked out for one another and had our highs and lows, with one another and our boy "crew." In Junior high, I became what I now Identify as depressed. I did not know what that was until then.

From time to time, I hurt my girls. The depression and (trauma) would manifest itself in such a way, I would go so deep into my thoughts and become super quiet. I am not sure how long this would last but when I would come out of the all-encompassing sadness, I would lash out at my crew and ask them why were they not speaking to me and, why were we not going to lunch anymore? Until one day they said to me gently, "Jennifer, it is you who would stop speaking to us. You would not want to be with us and ignore us," so we leave you alone until it passes." I remember denying it at times because, when I was in that state, I truly did not know that I was acting that way. Once I saw how kind they were to me and one girl in particular threatened to take her friendship away because I hurt her so. I finally was able to see and recognize when I was starting to go into that pit again. I even heard a friend of mine one day during class, say, "uh, oh, there she goes again." This was my cue to snap out of it! Especially if I wanted to keep my friends.

My self-esteem was at an all-time low. I was constantly told I was beautiful but all I saw was an ugly person. That message droned more in me than any other message especially when one of my friends whom "I loved" pushed me into garbage and slapped me so hard on my face that he left his handprint on my face and neck, all because I noticed that he was sad over an incident with his dad. He was super angry at me for mentioning it to him and decided the way to shut me up was pushing me into garbage.

I went home in a daze, beyond humiliated for what he had done to me. He was my friend, someone I trusted, someone for whom I had strong feelings for. He never apologized to me for it, and it took me a long time to forgive him for what he had done to me. When I went home, I looked in the mirror to see why my face was stinging, when I saw the imprint of his hand, red on my skin. I was shocked to see such a pretty face staring back at me. But that must have been a lie, the image I saw, for anyone who throws you in the garbage, you must be no good.

At another time, while at home from school, I was sitting on the couch, talking to God when all of a sudden, a feeling of dread came over me. I felt as if someone physically threw a heavy load on my head. It felt as if a bag of clothes were thrown on top of me, and since then I would have a feeling heaviness. I came to understand it was depression that came upon me. I could no longer just pray sadness away, not all the time anyway, and I would settle into a deep funk, that I wanted to get rid of. I knew the enemy would do that, so that I would always feel burdened and heavy with the weight of my problems; wanting to harm myself!

Around the age of 12 or 13, during my junior high school years, I became suicidal. I wanted to die so I did not have to feel the pain of not having my parents around, deal with my abuela's, mental and verbal abuse or live with the memories of being sexualized and wanted because of my body and face. I began thinking of ways I could take my life, so much so, that during a lunch break at school, I was with some of my friends, and we were crossing the street when I decided I was going to throw myself in front of a car. I told my friends I was going to do it as a cry for help. I began to slowly walk into the oncoming traffic, when one friend yelled at me and pulled me back and said, "No, Jennifer you are not going to do this."

They asked me if I wanted to get help, that they would speak to the teacher for me and get me some counseling, I became angry at them I said "no", but by the end of the day, my friends were not having it, and I wound up speaking to a crisis counselor. I was secretly grateful to my friends. I was deterred for a little while, yet continued to think of ways to harm myself, Like throwing myself out of the window of my apartment and other ways. My father's death at 17 prompted me to try my last suicide attempt a year later at 18. I was going to cut my wrists. Once again, the pain was just too much for me at the time and felt I had no way out, when I then turned to anorexia.

Anorexia, I decided to become anorexic, I tried to hide my body behind my clothes, I hated having a grown woman's body. I wanted to disappear, not be attractive to men. The anorexia was also a way for me to be perfect and control something since I was in control of nothing when I was at home. The effects of the anorexia on my body, skin, and hair happened quickly. I wanted to punish myself in this way and then I would not have the pretty, womanly body that men or boys wanted to look at or touch. I also became anorexic because it was the one thing I could control. I read up on why teenagers and young adults become anorexic. One of the signs was the lack of control in their lives or a controlling parent as well as a myriad of other signs. My friends began to notice that I was not eating and that I was losing weight. I worked my way up to just eating a Snickers bar and drinking some Ginger ale until eating half a bar was too much for me.

I was glad when they noticed. That meant that I was seen and not ignored. As a result, I decided I did not want to do this anymore. Not only was I hurting myself but my relationship with Jesus was important to me. I knew that I was hurting my body and sinning against the Lord. So, I struggled but made the decision to stop and slowly decided to eat again. It was a slow process, and I did not want to give up control at all or surrender, but I did.

About a year, later I decided I would be bulimic instead. I had seen one of my favorite actors, play the role of a bulimic. When I decided to become one, I was at another point in my life that I could not take what was going on at home. As serious as this disease is, I tried it for about six weeks, and quite quickly my throat began to hurt from the acids. My perfect teeth at the time, hurt and I had developed a warped sense of my body Image. When I looked in the mirror, the image looking back at me would become distorted. I knew I had to stop, or this was surely going to kill me.

That would not be a bad idea I thought, then I would not have to suffer anymore. I just hurt too much physically and emotionally to continue to throw up constantly. So, I slowly sought help through counseling to overcome this as I felt as if I were drowning in an abyss, and if I allowed it to suck me in, I would never come out. Within a few months, I overcame bulimia. The thoughts to return came back from time to time.

For about seven months, my abuela called me "stupid" no matter what I did or said. It would be "you, this, that, and the other, you are so stupid." If I tripped, I was stupid, if I wanted a second helping of food, I was fat and stupid. It might seem hard to believe, but I vividly remember about 7 months that she just berated me. Being called stupid all the time, did a number on me, and aided my already depressed state and suicidal feelings. I also remember speaking to some friends at school about it. The word stupid did not come to affect me anymore than it did my senior year in college when I was finally going to graduate. I had a melt down and an anxiety attack right on the stairs of my dorm room. So much so that I needed my friend to calm me down. she did not understand why graduating was having this effect on me. I explained that my grandmother's words were haunting me. When I was about 14 in junior high, she called me nothing but stupid all the time, and now here I was about to graduate. I was told that I was too stupid, trying to be white and would never graduate. My friend responded, "you should be proud of that." I said "yes, but… you just do not get it!" The tapes kept playing in my head of my grandmother telling me I was stupid.

Regrets:

I was in acting classes when my therapist explained that she believes in my talent and that I should try out for Julliard. She would give me the recommendation so that I could go and audition. I was beyond excited and wanted to do it, but my self-esteem and fear of rejection kept me from pursing it. This is one of my biggest regrets. I auditioned for "The Fame school", I prepared my monologue, Laura from the Glass Menagerie. Her character I most identified with, due to her disability and the pain she experienced. I also gained 20 pounds due to being so nervous to get into that school, that I bombed my audition. I believe that I self-sabotaged myself. I knew when I was done that I was not going to get into the school, and true to that, I got my rejection letter about 2 weeks later. I was devastated and then berated myself, that if would have sang instead, I definitely would have gotten in, but I was too scared to try again.

High School:

I met women who until this day, are still my friends. Some have fallen away; others are still around. High school was very uneventful for me. Nothing to report here, except for the horrible education I received in my non - nursing classes. I had good teachers for that. I was horribly insulted when my Caucasian English teacher had the nerve to teach the class, how to spell cat and other simple words. I was beyond frustrated. I wanted to learn not be humiliated. Other than the sub-par education, I enjoyed my vocational classes and was told by my nursing teacher that I would make a great nurse and had a great aptitude for it. I was proud to hear it. My grades were also 90's and 95's in science, nursing, anatomy, and biology but after high school, I decided to not pursue my nursing degree.

In my personal life at home… April 15th, 1986.

No one had a clue that my father was going to show up at my abuelas' house. I was surprised to see him when he wanted to speak to his mom and his sister. They went to my room to talk and closed the door. I peeked towards my room and wanted to know what was going on. This seemed serious. Next thing I saw was my dad crying and so was my abuela. I thought to myself,

I hope he is not here to ask my grandmother again for money and made her mad. That would mean I would not see my dad for a while because she would be livid and remind him that she was not going to give him anything. I also had other thoughts swirling in my head, but not in a million years did I think he would drop the bomb that he did that day.

My father left for a while to go to his "rehab" program so that my abuela could tell me what had just happened. I saw my abuela's face and she first explained that my father was going to live with us. I instantly felt joy but then ambivalent about it because he was going to take my room. Great! I love you daddy, but my room? Can't he sleep somewhere else? How long was this going to be anyway? My selfish thoughts were interrupted when my abuela said that he was sick. Instantly, I thought cancer. Ok, I will help my dad in any way I can. I realized he may die. No, not die, he had the Lecler constitution behind him. He will make it when my thoughts were interrupted again and my abuela told me it was not cancer, but HIV.

My head grew heavy, and I began to cry. My father was HIV positive, and he was surely going to die!!! Serious panic began to grow, and I did not know what to do. Shock, pain, and fear consumed me all at once. I wanted to lay down and die right then and there. I did not have my father for most of my life, and now he came home to die. With all these thoughts swirling in my head and a deep pain in my heart, just like that I resolved myself to be strong and not crack. This is what we do. We suck it up, put on a stiff upper lip and act like nothing has happened. Yep, strong is what I would be.

Not much was known about AIDS at the time, it was still new. All we had heard at the time was that it was highly contagious, and I wondered if I would catch it from just touching him? If I eat from his plate…? He was my dad. How could I not commune with him? How careful did I have to be? If not the same night or a few days later my dad was holed up in my room. This was going to be "my new normal." I would come home from school and say "hi" to my grandmother and then run to my room to be with my father. We would laugh it up for hours at a time like we were best friends or brother and sister. My abuela would come to point out that she was no longer receiving my attention and all of it would go to my dad. On the one hand she loved it, that we got a long so well and on the other hand, it was true. I did not want to speak to the cantankerous old woman. She surely was not as fun as my dad.

Throughout his 3 years with us, I saw him take over 12 medications to stop the progression of full-blown AIDS. Each medication was the size of a horse pill, and he had trouble swallowing them. All that medication he took was to stop his blood from reaching there. Until his platelet levels revealed he was now not just HIV positive but had full blown AIDS. He was already a skinny man as I had mentioned before, but towards the end, I could see his bones through his pajamas. This was heartbreaking to me. I had seen my dad quickly begin to lose his eyesight and need not just glasses but a magnifying glass to read until he could not even see with that.

My dad and I would take walks together, or I would accompany him to his appointments when I was not in school. On the way to such an appointment, this man began to argue with my father for no reason. His eyes changed color as if they were glossed over, and he began to punch and attack my father. I tried to get him off of him I even told the guy my father was sick, please do not hurt him. When I spoke to him, his eyes would return to normal. He would then look at my father and his eyes would gloss over into a yellow egg yolk color and would punch and kick him.

No one would help me until I asked him to get off my dad. I would come to realize that this man was demonized. I did not learn how to fight. I knew I had to pray, but in that moment, I was dumfounded and scared that this man was going to kill my dad. When I helped my dad up from the ground, the man had busted my dad's tooth. My father was bruised and toothless. We now had to go to the dentist. I felt incredibly guilty and asked my father to forgive me for not being able to help much or even pray like I should. My daddy was not angry with me, and when we went home, my grandmother told me that I could tell people under those circumstances that he was ill. I was crushed and scared. What if this happened again? What if they hurt him again?

I will never forget another harrowing moment when my father tried to take his own life. I not only had to worry that he could get into a fight in the street but now he was trying to hurt himself. My abuela and I were at home when I heard my dad crying and talking to himself. I look into my room to see blood on the ground and him slicing his wrists. He wanted to die. He felt he was going to die anyway! Why not just go sooner? My grandmother and I tried to stop him. As soon as I saw the blood hit the floor, I wanted to die myself. There is no way to describe what seeing your dad trying to take his own life does to a person.

I quickly called 911, and the cops came pretty quickly. However, as distraught as I was, the cops had no compassion at all. I did not know how severe my dad's injury to his wrists were or if he would accomplish his goal in front of us. So, calling 911 was logical. There was both a female and male cop. The male scoffed and asked me to call when there is something more serious going on. My dad apparently had a flesh wound. How was I supposed to know? All I knew is that my father was trying to kill himself and there was his blood on the ground. Can you believe the nerve of that cop? I told him as much, yelling at him for being so compassionless and telling me this was a waste of his time! When he looked at me like he was going to hold what I was saying against me, I backed down because I did not want to go to jail for yelling at a cop and being distraught at my father's suicide attempt. I was so angry and almost continued yelling. The cop's look stopped me.

During my father's stay, we would have many conversations about God and where he was going when he died. My father during one of those conversations cursed me out and told me he does not care where he was going. Who was I to judge, and what kind of Christian am I? Although it hurt, I still continued asking him when I felt led. "Where are you going to go when you die daddy? God wants no one to perish. But have everlasting life! Don't you want to live with Jesus, and be with God, where there will be no more pain or sorrow, where all you are going through in your body is gone?" Maybe it was me not relenting and not caring too much at times that he would become terribly angry and belligerent toward his own daughter. He finally paused to think about what I had asked, and then he would tell me to scaddle, but the anger subsided. It was not until an older cousin of mine came one day and began to preach the Gospel to him, that my father finally accepted the Lord as his Savior. Oh, what a happy day!

I questioned if my dad had really accepted the Lord as his King because I knew my father's mouth and how he had treated me in the past when I would speak to him about God and my relationship to Jesus Christ. They say you will know someone by the fruit they produced. My father began to show that he meant business and that he really did accept God and loved him. My daddy and I would read the Bible together, and when I would forget or get caught up in other things he would say, "it is time to read the Bible, Jennifer, come." We prayed together and he would ask for forgiveness for his sins. These moments were some of the sweetest times I spent with my dad. We would also speak deeply about different issues, and he would ask if God had forgiven him for the things, he may have said or done in the past? I would tell him that in John 1:9, God's word says that If we confess our sins, he is faithful and just to forgive us. This would bring him comfort.

My daddy had a lot of sick days, days where he would sleep and sleep or he would be in the bathroom a lot, sick as a dog. He had 3 major moments where he wound up in the hospital. I would come home from school and he would not be home. My heart would hurt deeply since I did not know if it were the last time I would see him, and he would not be coming home. He did the first 2 times. His 3rd time in the hospital, my grandmother and I were approached by a social worker who let us know we were to get ourselves, ready. My dad would need Hospice care. I did not know what that was. The social worker proceeded to explain what Hospice meant. Hospice was for patients that were going to die and did not have much time left." WHAT??? NO!!!", my daddy was coming home, he has made it out before! This lady did not know what she was speaking about. An indescribable amount of pain came over me. He was going to live... my God! I gathered myself together and once again decided I was going to be strong, there goes that word again, "Be strong!" I decided I would just put away the fear and pain as best as I could and be strong for my father, my abuela and myself and his brothers too.

I made sure to visit my dad at the hospital and kind of said my goodbyes early. I had asked him for forgiveness for offenses I committed towards my dad. I would be angry at him during his stay at various times and we had a fight or two, yet I did not, nor could I live with any regrets after he was gone. My dad let me know that he had forgiven whatever the offenses and attitude I had toward him. I know that I was not always nice to him. I had attitude about the things he had done in his life and not being there for me as much as I needed him, but if God had forgiven him, how could I not?

It is said in the Hispanic community that If you have a dream, and it is raining that a person close to you has died. I never believed in that... until I dreamt that there was a big rainstorm outside, and there was such sadness in this dream. A few days later, at 3:00 in the morning, the call came that my father was gone. My uncles were called, my aunt and anyone else who immediately needed to know. We then ran to the hospital. I did not know what to expect. So many emotions ran through me. What was it like to see a dead person? How would my dad look? I did not know the silly things you think, or the thoughts I would have at the moment. As soon as we arrived, my dad actually had a smile on his face and his upper body was warm. He looked at peace. I was glad to see that. I also wanted and hoped that he would wake up.

My father died during my Senior year in high school. After his death, I began to feel really tired. It was a fatigue that I had never felt before. I would come home and fall asleep. Next thing you know, I would be awake for about an hour, still feeling tired. I had never known this fatigue before, and my muscles felt achy. After being awake for a short time, my upper body would literally fall back, and I would not wake up for another 7 or 8 hours. I went to school, but on the weekends, I was like a zombie who could not get out of her slumber. It was not until I was preparing to finally leave for my first year at Nyack College that I finally learned what I was suffering from and how keeping all of my grief in about my father's death, made me ill.

College:

I started out at college in the city. I hated it. It was a school very much into politics. There was a lot of walkouts and lockdowns at the school. Having to pay for my education and then not being able to go to school because of someone else's radical views did not jive with me. When the students were not protesting. This is where I began to cut classes that were super boring. I wanted to be like everyone else and what I had seen on television. It was silly, but cutting class is what I did. I had 2 other teachers who had tenure, and so as a result of it, they decided that they would just put notes on the board and then leave class. No teaching just notes. Both teachers would show up 20 or 30 minutes late to class and then begin writing on the board. I was beyond frustrated. Some students and I went to their supervisors to complain and was told that they could do nothing about it. They had tenure. After about a year of this, I decided it was time for me to leave and instead of going to another CUNY school, I would leave and go "Upstate."

I was not ready at 18 to leave my home but going to the particular college that I went to in New York City, let me know exactly what I did not want. By the time I was 21, the opportunity to apply to several upstate colleges came into the picture and I began to do my research on Christian colleges. The now defunct Kings College which I believe was located in Westchester county, was the first college I looked at. My excitement began to rise, and I made an appointment to visit them while I was on vacation from my school. The train ride on the Metro North was wonderful. I surely hoped this would be my destiny to go to this school. When I arrived, I had to find admissions on my own. I was greeted by someone who seemed friendly enough. Yet, there was a coldness I felt in my spirit but could not put my finger on.

It came time to meet with the admissions counselor…I felt as if I was being interrogated instead of interviewed. It was brought to my attention that everyone who studied at Kings College had the best grades (I did not) and the best families, even the one or two token Latino and black students. I could not identify how I felt after speaking to her, but I knew I was sad, frustrated and confused once I left the admissions office. I had a feeling I was not going to be accepted there. Months passed and I had forgotten my experience with them. Now a good friend of mine wanted to attend Kings College. She was nervous and excited as well as hopeful. She asked me if I would accompany her, I said "yes." On our way up, we sang praises to the Lord and had a good time. However, when we stepped onto campus, I began to feel uneasy once again and so did she. As we walked to admissions, it all came back to me, my experience, being talked down to, the unfriendliness of those on that tiny, hilly campus. I did not want to ruin it for her.

When my friend came in, she was happy. When she left the interview with the admissions counselor her face was crestfallen. I began to ask her if the admissions counselor talked down to her. Did she say, you were not good enough, that your grades would never make it? My friend answered "yes" to every question and we decided to hightail it out of there and never look back. Not too much longer after that, the college closed due to some accusations of discrimination and other things. Not sure how long it took but I decided to then go to My Alma Mater and stay there for grad school as well. I believe I found out about the college from someone who attend there. I was intrigued and decided to pray about going there.

At one point, I had a dream about attending my Alma Mater and visiting it. When I woke up from this dream, I knew I had to schedule an appointment. I called and spoke with M.S. He was down- to- earth and made me feel at ease about the application process. He also informed me that they pray over every student and seek God on who should attend the school. Hearing that excited me. I thought this is definitely a good Christian school if they are doing that, praying for everyone. A campus visit for a weekend was planned, and off I went. I was told by the person who had attended the campus for a while that It was a party school.

When I arrived, I looked for the signs. I saw some things that made me question if this school would be a good choice but decided that it would be when I was welcomed by a guy on campus named Ernie. Ernie made sure he introduced me to people and showed me around campus. He even invited me to eat with a group of his friends. During my stay, he made my time on campus easy. I was still a nervous wreck and hoped that I would be accepted. I stayed in Christie Hall with a young woman who was not exactly friendly toward me but loved to speak. So I sat in the room and listened to her tell me stories about whatever she wanted to talk about. That night she decided that she would have me sleep in her room by myself and she would go sleep with her friend in her room. I was uncomfortable but glad to sleep by myself.

When it was time to go home, I left with the hope that I would be hearing back and admitted soon. I weighed the good and the bad I had seen and thought, I could handle this; I am ready. Weeks passed and then the call came. I would be losing about 24 credits from the college I attended in the city. But 16 credits would transfer. They prayed and felt that even though my grades were subpar, I would be a good fit and find support on campus. M.S. also felt God had a purpose for me to be at this college. So, he welcomed me aboard. I was beside myself with glee.

Now to tell my abuela, I knew that she was not going to take it well at all. When I had applied to the city school, my father had died just 10 months before. She let me know that she was not going to support me through college because she wanted me to work as a nurse. My abuela also became angry and gave me the hardest time when I let her know that in order for me to receive financial aid, I needed a letter stating that my father had not supported me or given me any money throughout his life. My abuela was so mean that it caused an even deeper trauma in me, and that is when I started to not retain information in my head after I worked hard to study for tests and finals. She cursed me as per usual and said I was ungrateful and deserved nothing.

Was she going to say the same when I told her I got into Nyack College? I did not think I could take anymore harsh and demeaning words towards me. My abuela was the only one who dehumanized me for wanting to go to college and not remaining status quo. So much in fact that she told me that I was "reaching too high above my fanny!" That is the pretty way of saying it. I remember her even arguing with me and asking me if I knew what I was talking about when I used words she did not understand.

The day came to let her know that it was official; I would be leaving and staying on campus. She did not speak to me for a few days, and then came crying to me asking me how I was going to leave her like this? She said I have always been ungrateful, and how can I go so far away from her? A girl is not supposed to leave her home until she is married. On and on she went. But it was crunch, time. I had about 2 weeks to find someone with a car to help me move on campus. My abuela went into action, she called around, and went around to people she knew from the neighborhood until someone finally said "yes." Even though I had done a bad thing, according to her, she helped, and I was proud of that. She really hustled until someone helped me.

Healing and Confrontation:

The day had arrived for me to move in. I could not wait to get on campus and leave my grandmother (abuela) behind. It was not a long trip from New York City, and I thought to myself, I hope she leaves quick, so I can be free. My abuela wanted to see everything. I was mean, and she got angry with me. When she finally left and I was left to unpack, all these angry emotions stirred up inside of me and God began to work on me. It was as if a mirror was held up to my face. This is when I heard God's still small voice say to me "This is where I will begin to help you heal and help you deal with your sins." I began to ask God, "Why? Why are you doing this to me? I have not even been here a day, I just got rid of her. I want peace!" I began unpacking and later that evening I was going to meet my roommate.

I had decorated my side of the room with pictures of me and my bestie from high school. I was not much of a picture taker nor did I liked to have pictures taken of me. When I finally met my roommate, she asked me who was the other person in my pictures, and I let her know it was my "best friend." My roommate proceeded to tell me that she thought I was the lighter - skinned one and did not want to room with me. Great, my roommate did not like me because of the color of my skin. She was Caucasian and did not even know me to judge me in any way, shape, or form. After her bold statement which hurt, I continued to be friendly toward her, but she did not care and decided to go to her friends' room to complain about me. Her friend had the audacity to come to me and ask if my friend, "the light - skinned one was coming?" because she would room with her. If not, she has another friend who might come back to school, and I would have to leave when she came.

I explained that I was not going anywhere. They could give me a new roommate and she and her friend can go somewhere else. I guess that made her angry, so for the next few weeks she proceeded to be rude, come in late and throw her keys on the desk, to wake me, make fun of me, have her so - called Christian friends bully me, by putting things on the door like toothpaste and Vaseline for me to find. I got wise and hip to her schemes and would avoid the traps she set for me.

Often times instead of fighting with her or giving her the time of day, I would cry myself to sleep, feeling dejected, defeated, and not heard. My friends at the school said I was too soft, and they would have hit her. I can honestly say I was well on my way to a physical altercation with her. There is only so much a person can take. However, guarding my testimony was my priority. Prior to that happening, I decided to discuss the matter with the Dean of Students.

The Dean of Students basically dismissed me and told me that as a 21-year-old, I did not have any idea what I like or whom I would want to room with. I pleaded my case anyway and let him know that at this age I knew very well who I would mesh with and whom I would not. It took some doing, but within a week or so, I had gotten a single room on a higher floor. I would no longer be harassed or so I thought because in my own personal space, I could do as I wanted, and no one was going to treat me badly.

The Resident Assistant and her friends on my new floor were not a friendly bunch. They would say "hi," and maybe a few words, but never really have a full conversation with me or others like me, meaning us dark skinned girls. They also thought I was 3 years younger than they were when we were actually all the same age, 21.

Forging friendships with different people in my dorm and the girls on my floor, did not take long, I also had some "guy" friends that I had made and could study and with whom I could joke around with. I had memorable moments, days, and weeks that have stayed in my memory bank for which I will always be grateful. I also began to travel a lot while I was at school through drama and music groups and visiting friends from school. Even with such great times, I always seemed to have a depth of loneliness and pain that seemed to be forever before me.

A train ride and a Diagnosis:

Freshmen tend to gain what is known as the "freshman 15." I, in fact, did not gain the freshman 15. I lost 15 pounds. I was happy at that turn of events, but it came from being sick. Just before I went off to Nyack College, I happened to be on the 6 train in NYC when I saw an ad that asked if you had symptoms, such as, low-grade fever, sore lymph nodes, extreme and unexplained tiredness and the list went on.... My eyes fixated on that poster. At the end of the poster, it explained that if you were feeling any or all of these symptoms, you may have Epstein Barr. I had every symptom. Finally, someone knew what I had been experiencing for months now. The extreme tiredness and sore muscles, that no amount of rest would cure. My throat always hurt and felt as if I was on the verge of a fever. It was awful. I would not wish that on anyone.

I made an appointment with my doctor and explained that I saw a poster that described all my symptoms and I believed I had Epstein Barr. The doctor ran a blood test and hoped I did not have it. I hoped that she had the cure as well. I was hoping to feel so much better. That is what doctors do, right? They cure what ails you? Well, a few weeks later the blood work revealed what that poster said I had. Epstein Barr! Now what? Since the diagnosis and the illness were still new to medicine, at least how to treat it, the advice was lots of rest, and stay in bed. Stay in bed??? I am going away to college, and I am busy these days with church.

At this time, I do not remember what else I was told to do but I finally knew what was wrong with me. Fast forward to school. I did not eat much because my stomach always felt bloated and full which were two more symptoms associated with Epstein Barr. I had low grade fevers and again the tiredness and body aches were prevalent. Off to class I would go and back to my room to sleep and study when I could not the other way around. When I did feel hungry, I would eat my regular food, or the cafeteria food and they would make my body feel worse. I relegated myself to eating tuna on crackers, cheese, and yogurt. I later learned that cheese and some yogurts I ate, caused the pain in my body so I stopped eating that as well. I mention all of this because it was a significant period of 3 years before I recovered. I would be on the verge of passing out on campus when I had somewhere to go or was walking into town which was down or up the hill to campus. I was dizzy all the time, and the exhaustion was unbearable.

When breaks would come in between semesters, I would go back to my abuela's house. All the stress I continued to deal with while there, added to my exhaustion. It was also during this time that my beautiful cousin came to live with us as an infant. One of my duties was to change her diaper. My illness became so severe that I would be done for the day at just changing my baby cousin's diaper. A wave of fresh exhaustion would wash over me and all I could do was sit or go back to sleep. I would cry when my grandmother asked me to go across the street to the supermarket, because if I did, I would be so exhausted afterwards. I could do nothing else for the rest of the day. Sometime later, I learned that all the trauma of holding my father's death in and trying to be strong all the time took its toll on my body. 3 years in fact.

Lessons to Learn:

There seemed to be so many lessons the Lord wanted me to learn in college. I always said and genuinely believed that God brought me to Nyack to heal, not for academics. One major lesson was learning to rely on HIM. It started with me wanting to hang out with a group of girls on campus with whom we were more than just acquaintances. We had shared many talks in our rooms, deep hurts, about God, so much. Well, this particular week for some reason they acted cold toward me. They had the chance to hang with the popular guy on campus and his friends. They flaunted the fact, so they wanted nothing to do with me. I was completely rejected by them. They had flat out stated that they had more important things to do and did not have time to speak with me. So, the ever-sensitive person that I am, I spent that week crying, trying to understand why God had allowed these girls to treat me this way? Why the rejection? When I had experienced so much already.

There was a campus service I was invited to that weekend and the preacher man at one point looked straight at me and told me that God allowed what happened with those girls, so that I may find my self-esteem in HIM. He held up his Bible and said," this is where you find your worth. Not in people." Wow, that Is why I had that terrible week, and I so wanted to find my self-esteem in God, but I admit, I wanted and felt that I desperately needed the approval, affection, and acknowledgement of others. On the other hand, I was upset that God would put me through that. It hurt like the dickens! Slowly but surely, I tried to work on not caring or wanting others to love me so much. That was a hard lesson to learn.

Show me the money!

Financial difficulties when one is attending school are a woe 99% of all college and grad students know. Not having the money, not enough financial aid, out of pocket expenses, ridiculously expensive books, and so on.... but God wanted me again to rely on him and know that if he wanted me to stay in school, he would provide. At this point, I just had no clue where the money would come from and was constantly afraid that I would have to pack - up and go home. I worked many jobs on and off campus. I was a babysitter and receptionist. I worked up to 60 hours a week while being a full-time student. However, it was not enough.

I would like to say that I always trusted and did not panic, but I did more panicking and choosing to be upset at God more than anything else. Yet, the Lord had mercy on me many times over. He would just have people, one of them being a boyfriend, pay for my Junior year, second semester bill. Professors, and staff were used to encourage me to look to the Lord and trust that he would provide for me, and one or two helped me financially as well. I am forever grateful to them.

Grad school:

I was berated for going to Graduate School by my abuela. My getting accepted and moving on campus had happened so quickly. I can understand her being upset; however, it did not warrant the next 15 years of unforgiveness. I left college in May and went home for 7months to finish a 30-page paper so that I could graduate that December. My abuela would not leave me alone when I was writing that 30-page paper, and it was hard to complete it while she was still mentally and verbally abusive, but I did it and became a college graduate.

Come January, I began looking for a job so that I could leave my childhood home permanently. I quickly found an apartment which was right across from where I went to college in the city the first time. I was just waiting for the job I applied for to come through. Unbeknownst to me, God had other plans in the works. It seemed that trying to live and work in NYC was one closed door after another. I thought quickly about going back to my alma mater and applying for jobs through their "job book." While on campus. I had gotten numerous jobs through there. I loved the area and the campus, so it would be a pleasant trip.

Vividly, I remember going to the job center and not finding anything. I was deeply discouraged. I conversed with God about not being able to find anything. What do I do now? I cannot go back and live with my abuela, I just cannot. As I contemplated what to do, I decided since I had traveled all this way, why not tour the campus, and go back to my old dorm? When I got there, I ran into a former college friend. As we spoke, she began to tell me quite excitedly that she got into Grad School, Seminary, and she was living on campus. I congratulated her and then I was not sure what was happening. When as she spoke about how she got into Grad School, my heart began to pound, and I became hopeful. That was it. I would apply to Seminary!

She began to explain the process of how to get in and with whom to speak to. I just knew the Holy Spirit was speaking to me. I left my old dorm with a renewed sense of hope after having so many doors closed to me. That was a Wednesday, I believe. As I left the dorm and made my way home, I began to panic. How was I going to tell my abuela? I knew she would disown me for sure. Mind you I had not even called the school yet. That was a nerve-wracking thought as well. What if I do not get accepted? Even still, I had hope again.

When I got home, I kept the information to myself and admittedly forgot all about grad school by the weekend. Monday morning came, and my abuela was getting on me for something. I started to feel angry, when like a ton of bricks, the conversation I had with my friend almost a week earlier came back to me. I then said, "oh, call the Seminary!" I did and after speaking with the dean for about 20 minutes, it was determined that I had to come in person that Thursday to have interview. I became excited again and nervous at the same time because I had to tell my abuela. I would worry about that later. Thursday did not come soon enough. I hopped on the bus and got picked up near the bus stop. I arrived and sat with the Dean of Students. He was friendly enough and asked me why I wanted to attend school? After much conversing he informed me that I was accepted and could move in that Saturday. "What, Wow!!! Really!!! Oh, my Gosh! I am going to Grad School!"

At home, I had the daunting task of quickly finding someone who could help me move onto campus much like my move to college. I thought of my ex-fiance'. He begrudgingly accepted to come up from Maryland to help me move. I felt bad, but I really had no one else, and I trusted him even though we were not together anymore. Now to tell my abuela. We were in the kitchen. She was cooking when I got up the courage to tell her that I was leaving that coming Saturday to go to Seminary. My abuela immediately got upset and I think she even told me that I was not going! "How did this happen?" she asked. I explained as best as I could what had transpired and that I was given the opportunity to go to Graduate School. My abuela turned off the stove and went to her room. I knew she would be angry, and she did not speak to me for a while.

The next day, she bursted out of her room to blast me with her usual speech, that I am a bad person and how I can do this to her. How could I leave her alone, first I go to Nyack and then come back to leave again? At this time, I should have been used to her diatribes, but I was not, and it hurt. I felt guilty for years to come for going away to school to start my own life, finally. My abuela barely spoke to me. She cried at times but mostly showed anger towards me. Saturday finally came. Hallelujah! Off to my new adventure of Graduate school! I knew college was what I wanted to do, and I was determined to complete it. However, I only dreamed of being able to go to grad school. Now here I was, dropped off at my new dorm. I loved it because it was a step up from a single room at my college dorm. I had a kitchen and could finally cook my own meals. I had to pay rent and be an adult.

My ex-fiancé had dropped me off, he stood for awhile after he moved me in, and we spoke about us and perhaps still having a future together. We had also spoken a few times on the phone, giving one another hope that we would get back together again, but that never came.

I felt that it was a great privilege to study and learn about the Bible so to that end, I had some good times and great classes that had an effect on me. In the best ways, learning about God and HIS Word was awesome. Some of the people I met are still my friends until this day! I was blessed to meet, fellowship and be friends with people from Japan, Korea, France, and other countries. I loved it. I love cultures. I got to taste and learned to cook great cuisines from around the world. I can make a good Bulgogi. It was tried and tested for authenticity by my Korean friends.

There were many gatherings in people's apartments, and we would have BYOM parties. Can I tell you how offended I was when I learned that It meant "Bring Your Own Meat?" I grew up in a Hispanic family, and (quien invita paga). Which means if you are the host, you cover the costs. You do not ask your guests to pay for their meal or bring one. Eventually, I had to get used the idea because it was the way to get to know people, and I felt lonely a lot. So, offense aside, I would bring something to the party, always.

While in school, I also began to travel more and got to live my dream of going to Italy, I worked a lot, more babysitting, and more nannying, on campus and off. I began to do house cleaning as well to support myself. That is how I paid my rent and utilities.

As always, and I say as always, because things just never came totally easy for me, I had some experiences that if I could go back and react differently or change them, I would. For instance, I was made to room with people with whom I did not want to share a room with. I was forced to be with a woman who was very odd and would go into my room without my permission. I am and was a very private about my space. I had a curtain up at the base of my door, a pretty lacy curtain, one because it was pretty, and two, because as a woman, I was not always dressed up.

I was in my own apartment so I would wear noticeably short dresses and shirts to sleep in. It just so happened that maintenance would pass by quite often or a male friend would visit so I needed a barrier between me and the front door, as one could see into my room when the front door was opened. This roommate told the Student Services Director that I put that curtain up to keep her out and not be friendly. As a result, he came to me and gave me this speech about opening up and not closing myself off, etc. I was so angry, how dare she?

Once I explained to the director why I had the curtain up, he apologized and realized that this woman had made stuff up about me. Things were not good between us. I was extremely uncomfortable around her and asked for a new roommate. She did the same. No one believed me about what she would do if they roomed with her. She found a new roommate and the same things this woman accused me of, she did to the next person and so on. I was not perfect by any means. I would stir the pot at times, as well.

I would love to say I was not discriminated against, but I was and when I first complained about being moved and moving in with her, I was told that they gave me that roommate (who was black) so that I could be "comfortable." I was honestly stunned and upset that I was being told that because if they knew me at all, she would know that I get along with all races and had my preferences to room alone or with someone with whom I had felt better about. It was to no avail, and I felt powerless to defend myself. I was the bad guy for being upset about the racist comment and being forced to live with someone I did not want to live with.

My Loves

My story begins with my first real boyfriend. The moment I laid eyes on him; I was awe-struck." Wow, he is gorgeous and beautiful," my 13-year-old mind said. He was also so talented as he was drawing Mickey Mouse and Donald Duck on the Board during recess. He was older than I, I could tell. He looked more mature than the guys in my class, a real man! He was drawing on the board and he caught wind of me staring. We locked eyes. I froze and wanted to melt into a puddle right on the school floor. I realized that he smiled and did not embarrass me or make me look dumb in front of all his friends. What a gentleman! That was all I needed, I was a goner and in love.

I remember asking about him and found out he was a senior. I remember thinking he will be gone next year. How sad. Fast forward to many smiles at me and "hi, Jennifer, how are you?" as we all exchanged classes in the hallway. His comforting smile always made me feel 10 feet tall. Cue the violins and hearts. One day, a good friend of his asked if I would like him to take me home, walk me that is, so we could get to know one another. This was just before the whole school knew my feelings for him. I jumped at the chance and said "yes, I would like that a lot." I tried not to show that it mattered whether he did or not, but I was doing back flips all the way home, figuratively. I am not sure how long after that conversation that he came and picked me up at my last class and waited for me. He greeted me, smiled, and asked me if I was ready to go.

I could not believe my luck. His friends and mine started buzzing around us and would not let us leave without knowing if we were dating. I was so mad and wished that they would just mind their own business. I did not want anyone to ruin this for me. However, he showed me that he could handle it and had the right words to say. We finally were left alone, and he was able to walk me home. Ironically, I learned how shy he was because he did not speak to me the entire 4 blocks until we reached my building, and we said a sentence or 2. We just looked at each other the whole way and would smile, like two dummies. A little frustrating but still sweet. He left and I felt a big ache in my heart. I wanted more time with him and wanted to get to know him better.

Two years passed and I ran into him near my building, he saw me, came up to say, "hi" to me and asked me where I was going? I let him know I was just going to the store to buy some gum. He asked if he could tag along? Of course, I said," yes," and off we went. We spoke about where he was going to high school and what I was up to, when we reached the store, he paid for my gum. What a chivalrous act. He also asked me if I wanted anything else. I think I said, "no," even though I wanted more and out we went back to where we met up to talk. I am not sure how we got on the topic, but he asked if I wanted to be his girlfriend. I replied "yes." Yahooooooooo!!!! It was my lucky day! The man I pined for, over two years, was now my boyfriend.

Weeks later, the official meeting of my abuela and His mom was underway. We were so serious. His sister let me know sometime later that he wanted to marry me and loved me. I am sure in many cultures meeting the parents is super important! It is in the Hispanic/Latino culture as well. We made dinner for one another and spent time with our respective parent. My mom even showed up for the dinner at his mom's house. Both parties approved of our relationship. I was on my way to dreaming of our future wedding, and we were seriously planning on joining our lives once I turned 21.

Every relationship has its ups and downs, for one thing, he made fun of me, my skin color, even though his mom was dark – skinned. He also compared me to lots of other girls he dated and would ask me often, "why did I not have this or that like this ex?" Those moments hurt me and lowered my already fragile self-esteem. I was pretty tenacious and felt that if he did not like me as I was, he could get to steppin.' I put up with a lot of his behavior because I had this martyr complex and felt that you just do not abandon people, sure they are not perfect, but he was pretty near to that, and so many other girls in his life also thought so. This was another problem, he was so handsome, he always had girls buzzing around him. He was not one to fend them off well and would let me know that even though he was not cheating, he could. Why would I want to know that? It got so bad that 1 year and half into our relationship, I just could not believe him and was nervous that he would or was seeing other women behind my back.

One thing I can say about him is that he was honest and abhorred lies. So, if he said he was not cheating, or he did not do x y and z, he did not. Yet, again, his view of "I did not cheat" was different than mine. Coming to visit me with lipstick on his neck, from someone else is not being faithful. I was always faithful and had no eyes for anyone else, except for my actor crushes. During a particularly good time in our relationship, it was a few days before Christmas, and we wanted to have fun. He called me the night before to ask if I wanted to go ice skating with him and another couple? I said "yes," although, I was afraid because I did not know how to ice skate. We were going to exchange gifts before we left. I could barely sleep just waiting to see what he had gotten me for Christmas and was hoping he would like what I got him. The next day, about an hour or so before he called, I started to get a funny feeling in my chest. Like we should not go ice skating. I was not sure why I was feeling this way. I did not want to disappointment him. He liked that stuff, adventure, and physical sports. He was a sprinter at his high school.

Well, he called to tell me that the other couple decided to go to her parents' home instead. I was disappointed and relieved all at the same time. I really liked this couple. Oh, well! So, he asked me "what would I like to do?" I struggled with telling him it was best that they did not want to come, because I had a funny feeling. He was so romantic and sweet about everything, I ignored what I was feeling so that I could give him the date he wanted. He knowing me, knew that I was hesitant about something. He asked me again, are you sure you want to go? I paused, feeling a bit of that heaviness, and said yes," let's do it."

Christmas day.

My boyfriend came over and he gave me the prettiest bracelet. It was delicate and gold. It really was lovely. He had also given me something else that I cannot recall at this time and I gave him his gift, it was a sweater. He liked it. If I am not mistaken, he asked me again if wanted to still go, we could go? We could go to the movies if I wanted or…. why did I say "yes!" Off we went. In my mind I thought ice skating would be a cinch, but Lord help me if I fall! The skates hurt me the moment I put them on. I wanted to take them off immediately. The blade almost sliced me because I did not know how to put them on without touching them. Then at some point, I lost my bracelet that he worked so hard for. He was pissed! I did not blame him. This must be the reason why I was not supposed to come. Look at all that has happened so far. Turns out things were going to get far worse.

We notified the guards to be on the lookout for a gold bracelet. Eventually I found it, but it was broken. He was unhappy but glad I found it. With my ankles hurting and losing my now found bracelet we decided to just leave and take a walk. As we walked out of the ice rink (good riddance), his mood lightened, and he became romantic and wanted to know if I wanted to take a long walk or go home the short way? I chose the long way. Deeper into the woods we went when all of a sudden, He stopped and held me in place. He started to shake, and I wondered what was happening? There in front of us was a teenager with an Uzi gun. Holding it at us. I began to get scared. The kid wanted to know if we had any money or jewelry on us. I looked at my boyfriend and asked him what to say? I lied and said," no." That is when he came toward us gun in hand and started searching our pockets. I instantly thought to myself," oh no, I just told him we do not have anything. He might just shoot us." The gunman did get upset that we lied. He made a comment about it, and I panicked even more.

The gunman found my bracelet and asked for my boyfriend's school ring among whatever else we had in our pockets. Then just as it looked like he was going to leave, he asked for my boyfriends' "letter" jacket. We both loved his Letter Jacket. I would wear it proudly to school and around my house. When he missed it, he would ask for it back. He did not want to give it to him. So, I pleaded with my boyfriend to give it up. Now was not the time to be stubborn. Oh, did I mention, he could be so stubborn! Ugh!!! Finally, I convinced him to give it up before this guy with the Uzi did anything. Once the gunmen got the jacket, off he went toward the entrance to central park. Praise God, he did not shoot us. Scared as heck, I breathed a sigh of relief and I wanted to get out of the isolated spot before he or anyone else came out to rob or shoot us. My thoughts of leaving got interrupted when my boyfriend who was a sprinter decided to take off after the gunman. I began to scream, "please stop, don't run after him," Help somebody! I was stunned when I saw that he almost caught up to him. Now they were both out of sight and out of the park. How could he leave me in the woods?

I started running towards the entrance when the 2 guards who were at the ice rink heard me screaming. I told them what happened and asked them to please go grab my boyfriend before he got hurt. As I said that I heard a pop! I stopped and began to cry. I screamed his name into the air and ran as quick as I could. Why was he a runner? Why could he not break his leg before he got to the gunman? I was out the park looking for him and praying the shot was for the other guy, not him. When I located him, a small crowd had gathered around my boyfriend which confirmed he had been shot. He was writhing in pain and asked someone to call 911. I checked on him and could see the bullet hole and his bleeding wound. I once again asked for someone to call 911. No one was listening. Instead, everyone was looking at me. I gave them a look that could kill, that the crowd literally gasped and took a step back. Someone then decided to call 911. The ambulance came and somehow, I got to the hospital. I do not think I rode with him. The ambulance people would not let me. When I got there, I wanted to know how he was. The doctor came out to tell me that he was going to live, but the bullet came awfully close to his heart. The doctor asked me if he should be the one to let his family know. I knew that it would come better from me because I had such a good relationship with them.

I nervously dialed the number. His sister answered the call, and she intuitively knew something was up and asked was it her brother? I said "yes," she asked what happened? I told her your brother has been shot! She screamed and began to hyperventilate; she was having an asthma attack. Great! Now I would have to worry about her too! I could hear her on the phone telling her mom that "he" had been shot, and she began to cry and asked me where he was? I told her the name of the hospital and about 20 minutes later they were by his side.

Once he was stabilized and his mom and sister saw him, I was allowed to see him as well. After a few minutes we were left alone, and I caressed him and held his hand. I began to cry and blame myself for him being shot. He asked me not to blame myself. I knew it was time to let him rest and go home. As I was leaving, he asked me to come back and give him a kiss, which I did. He smiled. I smiled, and off I went. When I got home and told my abuela what happened, she was horrified but glad that my boyfriend was going to be ok and that nothing happened to me. As I laid down to sleep, I cried and cried and cried, believing it was all my fault, the "Holy Spirit" had been letting me know that something was not right. Yet, he and I wanted to enjoy this date together and this happened. My boyfriend, on the other hand did not blame me. He was a gentleman about it through and through.

Months later, I had a nervous breakdown when my body knew that I was in the same spot where we were robbed, and he was shot. It was dark when it happened. Now daylight, instinctively, when I was at the very spot where all this went down, I stood in place and began to shake, and cry. I happened to be with a young lady who held my hand and told me everything was going to be alright. I was her camp counselor, and we were on a trip to the pool. That young lady was my anchor at that moment. Although I felt incredibly sad that she experienced that with me she was my rock at that moment. The child called the director and had her come over to find out what was wrong with me. That child held my hand and hugged me, then she was sent away from me and I was scolded for "acting that way" in front of the children. I was asked if I wanted to go home, or could I calm myself down? I was definitely not in a state of calm, so I opted to go home and was made to feel bad about that. I also did not really want them to know what had happened because I felt it was too private.

As I was dismissed and made my way out of the park, I began to get confused and pretty much lost my mind at that moment. I started saying that I was going to visit my boyfriend in the hospital. I had to see him. Mind you, this was 7 months ago, and he was long gone out of the hospital. When I "came to" as I call it, I made my way to his apartment, and his sister saw my state and asked me what was wrong, had I gotten into a fight? I said "no." She then asked," is this about my brother?" I said "yes" and told her what happened at the park. His sister begged me not to say anything to her brother as he was still coming to grips with what happened himself. All I wanted to do was see him, and make sure he was ok. I was not going anywhere until I saw him. Next thing I knew, he was walking toward the park bench I was sitting on smiling at me until he realized how upset I looked. Being the astute person he is, he asked me, "why I looked the way I did and asked me if I had been fighting?" I said "no." Then he asked, "Is this over me being shot?" I said" yes." He said "ok, what happened, they let you off of work?" I relayed the story to him, and he said well," let us go back to your job and explain why you reacted this way." I hesitated and fought a little telling him that it is private, but he aptly told me that he was the one who got shot so he will tell what happened.

We arrived back at the pool and my supervisor wanted to know why I was not at home and who was this person with me? He introduced himself and off they went to speak. I overheard her say that she now understands and to take me home, and for me to return after the weekend when I am better. Off I went in a daze. Not too long after my breakdown, he had one at a party and I had to be his strength and talked him off of a ledge (figuratively speaking). It was a tough season in our relationship. Yet, we soldiered on for about 6 or 7 months longer. He began to work a lot, and we had spoken of marriage before he went on to his next endeavor, but I wanted to go to college and get married at 21, not at 18. I broke it off with him after a year and half because I wanted to concentrate on my relationship with the Lord and felt that I had him on a pedestal, one that was more important than my Jesus. That had to be changed. We remained friends, I went away to college and him into the military. He would write and visit on my breaks. We then lost contact after my second or third year at college.

My College Boyfriend and Fiancé

I met my next boyfriend in one of the classes we had together my second semester. He sat in the back and was super quiet. I did not even know until later that he noticed me. There were a few Hi's and smiles on the way into or out of class, until one day, I got a call on the dorm room phone. "Hi it is… I am in your Philosophy class." I replied, "oh yes, the one who does not take notes and sits in the back of the class?" "Yes, Hi… Well, I wanted to know if you had eaten and if not, I am going to McDonald's. I could bring you something back."

Wow, I was taken aback, shy, and nervous. At the time I was suffering from Epstein Barr and not eating so much so I said "no, thank you, but that is sweet of you." After that call we began to speak more often and for a few weeks, a few times a week, he called me and asked me not to be shy or afraid that it would be his pleasure to buy me anything I wanted. At first, I was so not interested in him, but he won me over. I could also hear his smile when he called asking if I wanted anything from McDonald's, and I said, "yes thank you." He smiled and said "ok, I will be right there," hung up the phone and was at my dorm with 2 cheeseburgers a coke and fries.

I was beyond nervous but starting to get interested. Within 10 minutes he was downstairs at the lobby with the food when I came down to meet him. I do not remember if we ate together, but I think I ate some fries while we spoke, and he was happy to see me eating. If only he knew that was the first time in a long time that I felt like eating. I could go without eating for days during the height of my illness. Nevertheless, he promised to call me the next day after we chatted for a few minutes. He cared for me and was not after me for my body like most "guys." We would speak about my not eating and how concerned he was for me.

The next day arrived and the next, and I would hear from him at least 3 or 4 times a week. If I let him, he would bring me whatever I wanted to eat. However, even though he now piqued my interest. I did not want to take advantage of his kindness. He took me for rides and often to dinner to eat the biggest steaks I had ever seen. We officially began to date at some point and then the end of the school year was coming. He let me know that he would not be returning to school but instead would be pursuing his studies near his hometown. I was sad but eventually seemed ok by it.

Fast forward to my second year, the beginning of the semester when he came up in my thoughts, and I realized that I really had fallen for him. The details of how we became reconnected are a little fuzzy these days, but I remember being encouraged by a group of my friends to contact him.

    I believe I did, and he let me know that he also missed me, too. I was in his thoughts. My heart soared at knowing this and not being rejected by him. By the time we were off the phone, we had officially began dating again. Since our relationship at this point was long distance, he made his way down from West Virginia to see me every few months and came to pick me up so we could spend time together and see other places he wanted to show me. It was during this time that we discussed "our future" and getting married. He wanted to know how I envisioned things and where would I want to settle? A few months later, he began working at a children's home as a counselor. He was closer to New York than before. And made his way to see me more often.

    I missed him a lot and wished that he were closer to me. I was lamenting to a friend about missing him so much, she told me she would take me to see him in wherever he was. I was thrilled. Later on, I relayed that to my boyfriend and let him know how I was feeling. He decided that he would pick me up instead and take me to West Virginia, his hometown. I was excited. I also became nervous about the fact that West Virginia is known for having a racist history. How would I be treated, being that we were an interracial couple? My imagination ran wild with lynching and having racial slurs hurled at me. I had such a vivid imagination. It did not help passing by homes that proudly displayed the confederate flag. I even think one of those homeowners with the confederate flag caught a glimpse of us in the car and began walking up the hill to where we were about to pass. I could have been wrong and maybe my imagination was getting the better of me, but I know I saw a fist pumping in the air with anger saying something toward us.

    During the ride, he informed me that his mother would be coming to town and when I would meet her. I would also meet his uncle. We had a great time and lots of conversations on the ride to WV. He sang his favorite country songs, and I relished in the beauty of the WV mountains. Once we neared his childhood home, my nerves got the better of me. His uncle came out to greet us and instantly I smiled. I was introduced to his uncle, and he gave me a slight smile. I thought ok, not so bad. We entered his house and sat down. I believe we began talking about the trip, how we met, and things of that nature. Not so long afterwards, his uncle only spoke to my boyfriend and his uncle became very cold toward me, he began to make a few comments that gave me pause. Not quite crossing the line of racist but teedling there. This is when I went into defense mode. I was not going to let this man be rude to me or treat me any differently because he did not like my skin. As things started to get really uncomfortable for me, my fiancé told me it was time to go. He knew I was getting my dander up. So, we excused ourselves. Just as we were about to leave, my fiancé's uncle asked to speak to him. I thought that was rude as they went outside and left me in the house by myself. Surely, he could speak to him another time without me around.

When we left and were finally alone, my fiancé let me know that his uncle asked him if he really wanted to marry "a black girl!?" I asked him what was his response? He let me know that he loved me. I was a good person and would make a fine wife. However, he was concerned about "any future children." I was worried about how they would be treated, yet I was not as concerned about that as perhaps he and his family were. We seemed to reach the conclusion that God would help us navigate that when it arose, and that God would give us the grace to figure out what to say if our children were confronted with questions about their skin color or worse.

The next day, we met his mom. My fiancé had confessed that he did not have the best relationship with his mom. She left to go pursue her own endeavors and left him a teenager to fend for himself. She however was pleasant enough. I felt the silent disapproval, but she seemed to be a bit more open to "us." His mom also brought up the concern of interracial children and what that might mean for him and them. It was more as a caveat, something to really keep in mind and weigh in his heart.

J was set, he told me and knew that we would manage whatever came our way.

We had a great time in spite of my experience with his family. He showed me around, took me to his favorite spots, and we also toured an old fort, which was fun. After such a wonderful time in his home state and meeting his family who was less than enthusiastic about me, I settled myself that If this was the Will of God, I was to be his wife and he was to be my husband.

Once the trip was over, I began to miss him. The distance became of great concern, which weighed on me, he only wanted to speak to me once a week, since he was very involved in his work at a group home. He worked and had down time on Fridays after 10. I go to bed at 10 pm, so that was hard for me, but I made every sacrifice to wait for his call. As time went on, his calls became a little more infrequent and when I would get asked, how was I doing by my closest friends I would let them know that he does not want to speak to me as frequently as he once did. My "guy friends" would rip into him and said if you were my girl, I would never do that. A man is supposed to call his woman often, if not every day. Those words which I felt to be true only further hurt and confused me. Why does he not want to speak to me? I worked up the nerve one day to ask him and to let him know as clearly as I could that I need to hear from him more often. Our relationship was long distance.

At first, he would say he understood but then resort to the same routine of me not hearing from him, but for a 10 min phone call. He got to the point where he was so tired of hearing me ask for more attention and more time and he would allude to being ready to "answer the call of the wild." After one fight too many about him not paying me attention. He finally listened and once a week sent me a clue in the mail. He had made these beautiful cards that once received spelled out, "I LOVE YOU, JEN!" It was the most endearing and fun thing ever! Surely, he revived my love for him, not that it was gone completely, but I finally felt paid attention to and loved again.

That lasted a month or two and he was back to not really calling me. I was so hard on him, not just because of that but because of my expectations of what I believed a boyfriend should be. He did try. I felt so bad for the way I treated him at times. Yet, I was faced with these Ideals that I knew were not right. See, he was not "Rico Suave," he did not personify the "womanizing, Latin lover" image that I was so used to seeing and truly abhorred. J was handsome, had the bluest eyes and was tall, with a physique that certainly made my heart skip a beat.

He was sweet, funny, highly intelligent, loved God and really was clear on where he stood concerning marriage and what he wanted in his wife. He also treated me with respect and did not objectify me for my voluptuousness. He was so nice. I tricked my mind into believing that he was not very attracted to me at all. A warped sense of what I truly desired (which was a godly man) vs. what I grew up with messed with my mind very much. God brought this to my attention so that I would deal with it, confess it, and begin to heal my crazy notions. I was so hard on him at times and could not get over the simplest of things. This I know was hard on him. Over time we broke up and ended our engagement. I was heartbroken.

I last saw J when he dropped me off at seminary. He helped me move in. He asked for his ring back (my temporary engagement ring), and we had our last goodbyes. A promise to pray and see if things got better for us hung in the air…but it never did. He moved on and so did I, or so I thought. Months after he had gone, I sent him all our pictures of us together torn up into pieces and wrote a seething letter saying I was done with him. He wrote back and asked me to get help and returned my senior picture as I had asked of him. I was in so much pain over our break-up, more than I realized and took it out on him once more. I thought I was empowering myself because I wanted to forget him and move on. It took me a long time to realize that he just may have been the one that got away.

After him, I had guys interested in me, just not as much as I would have liked at the time. But there was one, 3 years younger than I, who pursued me much. I liked him a lot, but he was entangled with someone one else, and I was not a boyfriend stealer. He and I would hang out and pretend to study together at times. We would also fight because he would get on my last nerves. He asked me one day, to be his girlfriend. I wanted to say "yes," but again he was with someone else and I let him know that if I could not be his one and only, it would never be. Sometime later, he confessed that his relationship was over and a few other things, but I was not going to have it. So, the relationship never developed into much else.

I have finally found someone:

One of the major themes in college and grad school was "where is my husband?" "Is he here? Every time someone got together, dated, or got engaged, it was more than just another one bites the dust. It was, "why not me, where is my husband? When will it be my turn???" Well on one fateful day while I was in grad school, I decided to attend the singles' picnic at my church. As I got ready for it, I said to myself, "I wonder if today I would meet my husband!" I felt differently when I said it, as if it was to be. Then I quickly brushed the feeling away as crazy and kept it moving so to speak.

Once I arrived, I mingled, socialized, and was walking up to the grill where this blonde guy was cooking the burgers. He hid part of his face and seemed shy, so I decided if he wanted to play shy, I would make sure to find him and bother him later. Sometime later, I was sitting alone just enjoying the scenery when I felt someone sit behind me. At the same time, I said to myself, what happened to burger guy? I look over my shoulder and there he was. I then said to myself, "I wonder if that is my husband?" When those words were spoken to the air, my heart leapt and wanted to jump out of my chest. I felt the Holy Spirit tell me "yes, yes, yes, he is!" Quickly I looked around to make sure no one heard or saw what I did, and I dismissed it once again with a "Jennifer you are crazy! "Move on!

I kept my promise that I would bother him. I wanted to get him out of his shyness. I began by asking a few questions and began to get to know the blonde, blue eyed man. I do not remember at this time if this is the day that we learned we had a lot in common, and I invited him and another "guy friend" to come visit me at my dorm one day to watch movies. Fast forwarding weeks and months later, I knew that I had fallen for this man and his visits became more and more frequent. We forged a friendship based off of our mutual interests and realized we were falling in love.

The relationship was lovely at first but within a few months he started to try to break - up with me. Me having that martyr complex still, I once again believed you just do not abandon anyone. Even if they hurt you, you stick by them, and give them time to work things out. Even though my heart screamed break up with him, my martyr complex and love for him screamed louder. I would go back and forth, back, and forth, "with if this is how he is going to act, then I do not need to be with him". Again, I loved him! So, I was going to give him the benefit of the doubt. I also chose to ignore or mostly excuse away his mistreatment of me. He would talk about ex-girlfriends, whom he still seemed to have a thing for his "first' which freaked me out. Trust me I wanted better for myself and thought he is definitely a step above from anyone else I had in my life. If only he would just stop all of these things.

We dated for 4 years and got engaged and got married in 2002. One month to be exact before my wedding I was going to call it off. There were those "red flags" waving in my face. I was trying to gather the courage to break it off. What was I going to do with the gifts that had come in, the people who RSVP'd, my dress….? I don't know. I called a friend and told her what my concerns were, and that I thought I should cancel things. My friend advised me to pray long and hard before I make the decision. After some time, with the wedding just a few weeks away, I made excuses for everything and decided, "no, I want to be married. I loved him and with prayer and hard work, we will make it."

The Wedding:

It was a beautiful day! The weather was perfect, but there was a sadness within me that I could not describe. I was not able to afford the reception at a hall I wanted. Some people had ended their friendship with me once I told them I was engaged to him. I had 5 bridesmaids and was down to 2. The night before, I was unable to rest because I had to decorate the church basement. If it were not for my best friend who did a bang-up job even though she was sick and still helped me decorate, I would not have had a reception. People who had strict orders did not listen to me and decided to do what they wanted at my reception, The Bride and Groom's food, at the time, was taken. There was food packed for us to take on our honeymoon, and it was gone. We did not get any cake except for the slice you feed one another. Those were the bad things of the day. So, I thought.

However, the ceremony was incredible and turned out to be the ceremony I wanted. A couple of college friends did a praise dance, another sang. One person came from Long Island and rushed to get to my wedding because she knew I would be on time. Honestly, such a simple thing meant a lot to me. The photo session after the ceremony was fun, I had my friends, family and new- in- laws with us. My new husband was a diabetic. So, his crankiness after the ceremony was understood, but he started to become mean to me, and I was not sure why. I became upset at him for his strange and mean attitude and began to have an attitude myself. I did not want to be upset on my wedding day, of all days!

The reception and food, in spite of that, was good. My favorite part was when I participated in an old Hispanic tradition of putting Capias (Corsages) on people's clothes and thanking each one. My new family let me know that they thought that detail was very touching. Now it was time to go off to the honeymoon. I could not wait! He had a surprise for me. I think I knew and was hoping it was the place that I had wanted to go. After he ate, and I guess his blood sugars leveled he seemed to be in a better mood towards the end just before we left the church.

We arrived, and it was divine, I was so happy. It was the place that I had hoped it was for my first experience with my husband. We settled in and were both tired. I had a migraine since the reception but, ehem…being that I could finally do what married folks do, I was not missing the chance for any reason. He however was less enthusiastic and wanted to wait. WAIT!!!! I have waited MR. "este hombre tiene que estar loco si yo voy a esperar más tiempo…. (he must have been crazy if he thought we were going to wait any longer…)" We are not waiting, sorry!

So, we did what married folks do, and I thought to myself, it was worth waiting for the man that I loved and waiting until I was married. The next day, we left to go on to Canada. We had a good time talking about the future. Once we arrived in Toronto we checked into our place for the next few days, his attitude changed. I approached him lovingly and he pushed me off and would not hug or kiss me. That hurt. I asked him a private question and he outright told me absolutely not! I am going to bed! I was wounded but noted to myself that he did do all the driving, I should let him rest and then things will be better. Things never got better, I was left alone on my honeymoon for hours, even after he had rested for a while. He did not want to be with me, talk to me or any other thing.

It was now evening and having been alone to fend for myself, I began to write my "thank you" cards. Why not get that out of the way since my husband was not spending time with me. Once he woke up, we went out to eat, I did not know what to make of the situation, so when I came back to the room and he went back to sleep, I was on my knees crying out to God wondering what I had done wrong, and how could this be? I waited until my wedding day, and now I still cannot be intimate with the man you gave me? I do not understand. Why is this happening??? Here I was rejected, yet again. Not even a few days into my marriage. After crying for a while. I decided to go to bed myself.

The next day, things were a bit better, and he apologized. Mentally I was hurt but forgive and forget, right? So, we went out to have fun. I was hopeful again that things would be alright. The rest of the honeymoon was "hit or miss" and there was not much of anything but exploring Canada.

Once the honeymoon was over, and we arrived at home, I had fun unpacking all the wonderful gifts and cooking with the things that were given. Setting up home was fun. There were good moments and honestly just being with him was fun. I was not alone anymore.

Two months later with little affection here and there, I once again was left wondering what was wrong, was it me? Was it something I had done or had not done? Let me tell you, I tried it all. I prayed constantly and communicated with him about how I felt and how not having romance made me feel. We set up a schedule, among several other things, and he would talk a good game, apologize and then nothing would happen. I would buy into his words; I had no reason to doubt him. He was a Christian. He loved God, why would he lie to me?

4 years into our marriage before what I call, "the big explosion," there was still hit or miss times on the intimacy level. One particular evening, when we came home from work, he lost it over something I said, took my phone, and threw it until it broke in half and I ran out of the car to the neighbor's because I was scared of him. (He had never acted this way before.) My friends asked if they should call the police? I said "no." He was at our house and later came over and stated that he was ok now, I could come back. My friends asked me if I needed them to come stay with me while we talked. I said, "no" and walked to the house, while I prayed that things would not end up worse.

He calmly explained how he felt and what happened. We talked and then went to bed, with me still cautious but hopeful that this would not happen again. What did happen not too long after that was a year of abuse, mentally and verbally. He had refused to eat anything I cooked for him, he would throw the food I made, curse at me, and call me names. It was then that as a remedy for my pain,

I learned how to bake and stood by my old standby of coping: Overeating. I gained 40 pounds in 2 months. No exaggeration. Literally for one year, this cycle of abuse continued. I isolated myself, ate, baked, went to church, sang on the worship team, or came home and barely spoke to my husband because he would begin to berate and curse at me. I would go to work, be depressed and quiet, struggle because of the weight gain, rinse, and repeat.

Until the thought of divorce crept in…Oh, no! As a woman of God, I could not think of that. God would hate me because he hates divorce. I berated myself for thinking such a thing, but I knew not what else to do. How could this continue? I could not take it and decided that maybe I could go back to my abuela's house, live with her, get a job, and make enough money to get my own place. I would be fine.

No one should endure their husband treating them like this, even though I knew that other women had been through and were going through much worse. Yet, I could no longer take it. I asked him to get help because something was seriously wrong, I believe he already knew what, but I did not. We went to the doctors together, and he was diagnosed with Bi-polar disorder. Ok, so something was wrong. What would be the solution? "Medication" he was told. I let him know I stood with him and encouraged him to take his medications.

On the medication he was 10 times better, hardly any moodiness, and the abusive behavior stopped, until I would notice that a few weeks later all the abusiveness would come back. A snide remark, a roll of the eyes, I would let it go. After awhile I learned, he would stop taking his medication and that is when his terrible behavior would return. It was cyclical. 1 month on, 2 weeks off, 1 month on, no refills, up and down! It became emotionally exhausting. I recommended counseling…to save our marriage. He responded positively, and off we went. We got some great techniques that I knew would just work through hard work and prayer, but it was more of the same, up, and down, back, and forth, intimate today, no intimacy for months, nice, fun, kind, mean, abusive, the next. It was a pattern that until the day I said NO MAS!!! was a constant in my life.

I just did not understand, and for the last 4 years of my marriage, I would beg God to get me out; help me leave and make it on my own. I just cannot do this anymore. I became more and more depressed with the passing time. I was always serious and was told that I do not smile. How could I? My whole life was imploding before me. I was on the way to ending my marriage, all the while thinking and telling myself I was the worst person in the world for doing so. 8 months before we separated. I had just been through him wanting to kill me, He pretended that he was going to drive us off the road and crash the car, just to scare me. However, I was never too sure that he would have done it. I think he would have. There was one more incident where he wanted to kill me as well, but to avoid that he went to our guest bedroom and cried. While I stayed in the living room, frightened. I prayed and began to think of an escape plan.

Even throughout all 8 years of my marriage; he had mostly left me alone. At times we would sit together and watch tv or speak about various things. Towards the end, he would not even speak to me. After all those years I think that crushed me the most, not being spoken to. When he came out of his funk, I let him know we were done! He did not want to accept it but when he did, he almost seemed relieved. Not going to lie, he had moments where he would ask me to stay and work it out, but I was done. 8 years to long had crushed my soul to the point I thought I was dead inside.

It took me awhile to not feel dead inside, years in fact. I slowly, very slowly started to come back to life. Before then, I could not worship. I could barely pray, did not want to read the Word, or seek God, but I had no one else. Very few people understood. Most people unless they have experienced some form of domestic violence really understand the dynamics and the complex emotions involved or how long it takes to heal. Many people will tell you that you should be past it after a few months or even a year later. Healing has no timetable. Needless to say, I was devastated it was over, yet slowly and finally began toward my journey of peace.

Coping mechanisms and dealing with trauma

I had to deal with so much throughout my healing journey. The ending of my marriage: being divorced; being told that your destiny was destroyed: guilt heaped upon me, verbally and mentally abused, always scared of what was to come. Then dealing with my molestation and rape. There is no way to seriously describe what being raped and molested by the people you love does to you. It is soul wrenching, heart crushing. There were many times I felt debilitated, crushed by the weight of having to carry this all alone. A friend of mine recently described it as being in a horror movie, looking at it from the outside and seeing what is happening to you and not being able to stop it. I admit that when she said that it really resonated with me.

Except for friends and a few people in my church who knew what happened to me, there was not very many people I could trust. Being at home with a verbally and emotionally abusive grandparent was just too much to deal with.

I felt degraded and for the longest time felt like I was scum of the earth. You believe you are not even worth the ground you walk on. It was a horrible and heavy load to carry, and I know that many still struggle and feel this way.

So much had changed on my end as a result of the trauma. I was once good at math and then got yelled at by a math teacher and was unable to understand math as I once did. When I would visit my father "upstate," I would wet the bed. I did not have that experience anywhere else but there. That warranted a beating and shaming a couple of times from my father's wife Mami Ellie. G, my father's Caucasian girlfriend, was sweeter to me concerning this, I knew she was frustrated to have to change my sheets, but she still was much nicer to me and even covered for me with my father when I wet the bed one time. I remember he would also get upset with me, but I suspect G knew something was up.

I coped with my trauma by overeating, so much so that it became debilitating. At one point, I would eat until my stomach hurt. If I did not feel that way, I would continue eating. I berated myself time and time again for being so gluttonous. Yet I knew it was only because I was hurting. Yes, I liked food a lot, but I used it to hurt me, not nourish me. I wrote a poem when I was 13 about how eating was my summer's blanket, my warm breeze….

In college, due to all the mental and verbal abuse I was still receiving, no matter how hard I studied, I would blank out during tests and forget everything. So, I had difficulty with some of my studies and passing tests. I wondered what was wrong with me and if I were damaged goods or always would be. The trauma of all I had endured affected me much.

Rejection:

I was a "latchkey kid" and would be left alone after school or on the weekends when my grandmother had to work. When she came home, I would throw myself on her and because I had felt so alone, I would often times be scared that someone would try to come into the house. I knew that people, including me, needed personal space, but I was so happy that she was home and now I would not be alone. She would throw me off her so hard that I would land by the wall behind us or the next wall. That action alone deepened my pain, the rejection I felt and the loneliness, I felt throughout most of my life. Loneliness had been and was my constant friend.

God wanted me to find my self-esteem in HIM and in his Word, no one else. The Lord let me know that he allowed those girls to reject me so that I would seek HIM. After so much rejection in my life, I wondered why he would do that and have them outright reject me. It was a very painful, dark, and hard lesson to learn, A lesson that has taken me years after that experience to learn. Presently, I can honestly say that the older I get, and the way God's Word has been opening up to me lately, my self-esteem is not 100 percent, but I have reached a point that I love myself and know that God loves me beyond measure.

Protection:

I could fill a book with all the ways God has protected me throughout the years. One night I was coming home from Youth Group when there was gunfire not even 3 minutes from where I had just walked. If I were there 3 minutes more, I would have been in the crossfire. I have been chased and followed by different men throughout the years and threatened to be raped and killed because the person or people thought I was beautiful. Almost robbed if it were not for the elevator closing quickly and the robber not being able to open the elevator door. Men have purposely scared me just to get a rise out of me.

In high school coming out of a nursing assignment, 3 of my girlfriends and I were confronted by a man in his car. He cornered us with his car and tried to kidnap us. I tell you, there are more of these unfortunate events and stories, yet God has protected me through it all

Persecuted for my faith:

"Prostitute" and "whore" who worked on 42 street were just some of the names I was called because I was and am a follower of Jesus Christ. The city college that I went to, is where I heard these things. Professors would say things to me to offend me and my faith. One day, God helped me, and I was able to defend myself against the professor who tried to humiliate me in front of the class. Needless to say, I shut her up! She never mistreated me again for my beliefs.

My classmates watched me closely to see if the "good Christian" girl would mess up or stop following Jesus. I was being tested for my faith left and right. The class and I were going to a museum for an assignment when the train was in the station and everyone began "jumping the turnstile." all eyes were on me to do the same. I will not lie and say I was not tempted to do the same since I needed to be with the class to complete my assignment and was afraid to go alone. I quickly got a token and ran unto the train, that was a test, be it a tiny one. Once I got on the train everyone breathed a sigh of relief that I did not do the wrong thing by jumping the turnstile and my testimony remained intact. So much so that student that called me a prostitute, stated "the Jehovah's witness did good"

Silence is a killer.

One of the things about being abused in any manner, especially being sexually abused, is stun you into silence. I learned in my own circumstance that being silent hurts and often perpetuates feelings of shame. Silence was perpetuated in my home. I was always told that what goes on in my family, stays in the family. Amongst ourselves there was even the "that is none of your business" talk all the time. My family would be angry with one another If someone asked even the simplest of questions. Yet, I was different. I cut to the chase and like to get to the heart of the matter. Not everyone likes that.

When I had that dream at 18 about my grandfather's abuse… not at first, but as time went on, I could not keep silent. Being silent was stifling to me. I slowly and prayerfully looked for my tribe and began telling them one by one. Most of these people included strangers who would share their stories with me, youth counselors and trusted friends. I had to tell my grandmother, I wished I did not have to. In spite of her blaming me for not telling her sooner, a heavy weight was lifted. It was crushing me to keep it inside. The more I understood that it was not my fault. That there was nothing I could have said or done that warranted my abusers taking advantage of me, hurting me, and taking my innocence and childhood. I began to speak out more.

Once you are able to get to the place where you know that you did not deserve what you have been through, and that there is a God who saw what happened, you owe it to yourself to not be silent. I am not saying go out and tell the world, but if you believe that is what you need to do, then with God' help, speak on your own behalf. This is not something that happens overnight. If you so feel led, choose someone who you know is trustworthy and let them know, only if you feel you can. I know for some it could be a dangerous situation, so please use discernment and caution. Personally, I needed to get what happened to me out, and being believed by the people I trusted meant everything to me. I felt less and less ashamed and stopped believing that it was my fault or that because it was pleasurable at times that I was a bad person. It was one of the ways God used to help me transform my pain.

Another way God helped was by showing me that forgiveness, forgiving my abusers, especially my grandfather, was not for him. He was not going to win by me doing that but rather, it was to release me. Before God got me to that place, I fought long and hard to hold on to my justified anger and pain. He raped me, hurt me, took away my innocence and made me feel things no child should feel. I had every right to hate him or just be glad that he was gone. Yet again, over time, as I would bring my pain to Jesus, he graciously and lovingly let me know that I needed to forgive him and everyone else. Once I did, I experienced a freedom that I had not had. Months later, I admit I wanted to go back to the anger, though weighty and very heavy, it took some more time for the pain to completely dissipate, but letting go of that anger, and unforgiveness was uplifting.

"Bring it to Jesus" was a song I sang in Church at the age of 16. It is one of my favorites and everyone at church loved the song. God has always transformed my pain by my bringing it to HIM. Talking to HIM, letting HIM know the "good the bad and the ugly" of how I feel or what I am dealing with. That I did not feel like a Christian because of x y and z, or that I was harboring jealousy or anger towards someone and so many other things. Bottom Line, I tell Jesus everything. He knows it all anyway. I also wanted to build more intimacy with my Heavenly Father. There is no way to explain what is like to speak to someone you do not see but know and believe is there for you, NO MATTER WHAT!!! I have said some ugly things to the Lord, and he is still here to this day.

Even when I walked in the valley of shadow of death and feared. He was with me! He comforted me, he protected me, and he spoke to me and more than anything he still loved me. Many of us did or do not have someone to hear our deepest darkest thoughts. Most would shun us and say, "see you later" if they knew. But not The Lord Jesus Christ. He is the friend who truly has stuck to me closer than my earthly brother, Talk to HIM. Let him know what hurts, who did it and what you need. He will not let you down. He is also there for the fun times and what brings you joy.

The Word of God states that "though my mother and father forsake me, he will pick me up with everything he has." Psalm 27:10.

Post-Traumatic Stress disorder (PTSD):

When I was told that is what I had, I thought to myself that could not be! Only solders in the military get that! I am a civilian. Everything that was described to me that day with my counselor had my jaw dropping to the ground. She described me and my symptoms to a tee. Every time the memories came up, of the sexual abuse, and of a babysitter's son wanting to do inappropriate things to me at such a young age was very traumatic. At the same time, I was dealing with the constant mental and verbal abuse and being abandoned by my mother and father.

I had Flashbacks....

I developed agoraphobia and did not want to go outside anymore. I became fearful of being harassed or cat called as I often was. At the height of dealing with the rape, I just felt vulnerable all the time and could not take being looked at or lusted after. I was afraid of everything. That lasted for about 2 years. Flashbacks caused me extreme stress. On top of it all I also developed anxiety attacks.

The anxiety attacks were a whole other animal that paralyzed me with fear and rapid breathing where I would hyperventilate. It even got so bad that I thought I was going to die and not wake up or at the very least pass out from fear and stress. So, I isolated myself as much as I could.

Recently I just learned that anger is also a part of PTSD. I was surely angry a lot. My friends would say this is true.

Still Standing

Perhaps some stories deserved more details and a more in-depth look. There were also so many other stories I could have told. However, I wanted to get into the crux of why I am still standing and why I never ended my life. Bottom line, if I had not had a relationship with the Lord Jesus Christ, I would have never had made it. Having a relationship with Christ is not easy just like any relationship you have. There are ups and downs. The ups and downs are 100 percent due to my fickle nature. God never changes. He has remained the same yesterday, today and forever more. There were many times during this healing journey that I was so angry with God that I wanted to abandon my faith, or I would be half in and half out. What the Bible calls being Lukewarm. God's love was strong enough that I would run back to the feet of Jesus.

It was important for me to get to know the person of Jesus and who God was because my earthly examples were seriously flawed, as we all are. I am nowhere near perfect in any way. I needed the right perspective on God or else I was going to abandon my faith. Through spending time in prayer and just talking to God and reading his Word, I learned that God is not an abuser or the old man with long white hair, pointing his finger at me in blame or disgust as I was often treated by my earthly examples. I learned that he genuinely loves me. He was not and is not manipulative and he has never bullied me. Yet, I could not reconcile for a long time the loving God vs. my abusers. It took some time, years, to come to trust HIM and understand that he only wants good for me.

Sometimes along the way, I crawled to God, lying there in my wounds, broken, bleeding and bruised, wondering how he could let "these" things happen to me. Other times I ran as fast I could to the feet of Jesus, letting him know I needed HIM desperately in those times. God would extend his hand of mercy to me. Experiencing firsthand that he is there even in the worst of circumstances and loved me deeply and wanted to heal me. Where else do you find a friend, relative or loved one who truly would stick with you, when you are deep, deep in the valley?

When you are so soul tired and can barely form words to speak. Most people, though they try, get tired at some point of someone who always seems upset or is still dealing with painful and traumatic situations but not God He walks and has walked every step of the way with me, holding me in the palm of his hand, to ensure I do not fall or slip away. That is the God I serve. One of the greatest and impactful things God has stated in his Word is that he will never leave us nor forsake us. That is powerful to this woman right here and to that little girl inside who experienced so much rejection and abuse. My God, he is still here! He never left. No one should say the things I have said to Holy God, in my deepest pain and anger, yet he has forgiven me and picked me right back up. He is surely waiting to do the same for you. Let HIM and begin to receive that soothing balm, not just out a band aid on your wounds. He cleans them and lovingly makes sure you heal. It is not easy, but HE is worth it. I love you Jesus!

I learned that God is a friend who sticks closer than a brother. He is my provider, my healer. The Word of God also states that he binds up our wounds. He is the lover of my soul.

Present Day

My grandmother with whom I have had a volatile and love hate relationship with for so long is ill. 4 years ago, as she began to decline. I had to make sure that I have truly forgiven her for the 4 years prior and all the years of verbal and mental abuse that lasted up until 2013. Knowing that I have forgiven her for the pain, unkindness, and mental abuse that I have endured well into my adult years has been a weight lifted off of me. Due to her incapacities, I am unable to continue to hold anything against her. I cannot forget because the remnants of the abuse still linger; however, as God has healed me and continues to do so, it becomes less and less about what she did or how she was. Instead, I can say I love her. I could not say that over the years. I knew I did; it was just that loving her hurt.

These days it is about how she is doing and making she sure she is ok. Her health once again recently declined, and she may or may not have much longer on this earth. The family is hanging on by a thread just waiting to hear.

Current circumstances led me to leave the area I love to find peace and solace with my offspring in a different environment, and God has blessed me beyond measure. I admit that many times I often thought I would never heal, there was just so much to get past, so much to work through. Yet, I have taken one step at a time, and looked at the hard things and presented it before God over and over and over again, as often as I needed, even when I felt guilt or was told that I was being immature, to get over my hurt, get over the abuse because that was such a long such time ago. I still stayed in the trenches. Trust me, I do not mean to make it sound as if this is an overnight thing nor that I am all healed and do not need any more healing. Jesus has dealt with me where I was at and with what I needed at the time or moment. Sometimes willingly and often times unwillingly.

Growing in my relationship to Christ on the road to being a mature person, who is not always full of pain, carrying a backpack full of baggage all the time, meant everything to me. Along the way and along the journey of transforming my pain, I have paused. I have berated myself. I said to myself," you will never make it." I treated myself worse than an enemy. I would crawl into a hole. I would treat people horribly, oh, my journey runs the gamut. Then I would remember my goal, my desire, my deepest wish to transform my pain and not have it always consume me or break me further and that is what God did and has continued to do, transform my pain.

A Word of Encouragement and the Gospel

For those of you who have read my book and are curious about this Jesus and God I have mentioned throughout my book, I want you to know that there is no one in Heaven or earth that you would ever find as amazing or incredible or trustworthy as HE. The Lord loves you so much and he says that you are worth it, so much so that he died on the cross for you.

What that means is as the Bible says In John 3:16 "For God so loved the World that he gave his only son Jesus so that whoever believes would not perish but have everlasting life."

Romans 3:10 states that "There is no one good, not even one!"

The Bible also says in Romans 3:23 that "We have all sinned and fall short of the Glory of God."

But…

Romans 5:8 states that "But God demonstrated HIS own love toward us, while we were yet sinners Christ died for us."

He also says in HIS WORD,

Romans 6:23 states that "The wages of sin is death, but the gift of God is eternal life in Christ Jesus our Lord.

Romans 10:9-10 states that "If you confess with your mouth that Jesus is Lord and believe in your heart that God raised him from the dead then you shall be saved!" "For it is with your heart that you believe and are justified, and it is with your mouth that you profess your faith and are saved!"

To that end, we are all in need of a Savior, the person of Jesus to keep us from eternal punishment.
If you want to come into a relationship with Jesus Christ, yes, a relationship not a religion. You are welcome to say this prayer:
Dear Lord Jesus, I know that I am a **sinner**, and I ask for Your forgiveness. I believe You died for my sins and rose from the dead. I turn from my sins and invite You to come into my heart and life. I want to trust and follow You as my Lord and Savior. Amen.

https://en.wikipedia.org › wiki › Sinner's prayer

If you have prayed that prayer it is important that you find a Bible believing church and like- minded believers.
Please seek the Lord while he may be found.

For believers

God is our ever-present help in times of trouble, Ps 46:10 says. We know that our walk with Christ is not an easy one. There are so many hills and valleys to climb throughout our walk. I have been angry with God for years and years on end, thinking since he is God of the universe, why would he allow me to go through the things I have been through? More so how does he expect me to get through it all? Many days, it has been moment by moment and second by second. I have said to Jesus, "I am hanging on by a thread, and I am about to fall off the cliff, please come rescue me." In saying this, I have come to a place where instead of running away from God, I run to him. I have too, I have been facing some insurmountable difficulties. If I just have to hold on to the hem of his garment that is what I do, until he gives me the strength.

I have wanted and needed to transform my pain because the road I could have taken and struggled not to go on was total destruction. During my teenage years, the boom of teenage pregnancy had hit. I had not been intimate in that way with anyone so, no chance of that unless it was the immaculate conception.

However, the girls around my block made it seem so nice and cute. It was something the group of them were talking about doing, kind of like a pact. I wanted to be loved and love someone, so I am not going to lie, I contemplated getting pregnant at 13. I would talk myself out of it, and was very judgmental toward those girls, "who made it look so cute" and then the next day I would be like well maybe if I did the same, I would get the attention too and also be loved. Children had to love you, right? I know, silly. Silly as it was, it was something on the table at times.

The other thing that was so prevalent in the "projects" and my family was drugs. I can admit that I was not really tempted to get into drugs as I saw the destruction it brought to my family. The effects of it and the toll it took. Certainly, after my mother decided her "drink" was more important than me and my sister eating, crying from hunger. Begging her for spaghetti and meatballs. Made me not tempted for drugs. That was one hurt that took a long time to heal. To hear your mama, say, "this is my last 5 dollars I cannot feed ya. I need my drink," was not easy to get over. There were times during my suicidal days I thought about, going, and smoking marijuana like everyone else, saying to heck with everything and everyone. If no one cares about me, I do not care about me. Except for puffing 1 cigarette due to peer pressure and smoking half of 2 other cigarettes my whole life, I have chosen to stay away.

I also know that I would not have been here to write this if I had given into the suicidal feelings that I struggled with during my teen age years. The sexual abuse was enough to bring me under. Being raped and having that memory pop up at 18, left an indelible mark on me, but it did not nor has it defined me. Being sexualized at such an early age, being mentally and verbally abused, rejected for no reason by many people, throughout my life, living in a mentally abusive marriage, and having that dream end, losing my dad at an early age, having Epstein Barr, and recovering for over 3 years, racism, betrayal from friends. Has all been part of God transforming my pain.

Blessings

My Friends, I pray that my story has blessed you, and that you allow God, my friend and Love transform your pain. Please keep in touch and stay tuned for the Spanish version of Transforming my pain, Transformando Mi Dolor!

Now he that is able to keep you from falling, and to present you faultless before the presence of his glory with exceeding joy, To the only wise God our Savior, be glory and majesty, dominion, and power, both now and ever. Amen.

Jude 1:24-25.

Keep In touch

Email: Transformingmypain.com

Facebook: Transforming my pain

Instagram: Jennylec1

Website: Transformingmypain.com

Authors Bio

Jennifer Lecler was born in Spanish Harlem or as it is called in Spanish, "El Barrio." She graduated from Nyack College and got her B. A. in Psychology, Then her Master's in Professional Studies with a concentration in Counseling. Jennifer has also acted in various stage productions, sings, and does Voice Overs. In addition, she loves to travel, crochet and read.

    Jennifer was an Educator for 11 years, and still hopes to be a certified Teacher in the future as the Lord leads, by earning her second Masters in Education. Her experiences as you will read in her book, has shaped her, and constantly led her back to the One who not only saved her but the One who loved her before she was even born and continues to love her unconditionally, without reproach. Her hope is that you experience the same and that you the reader allow God to Transform your pain.

www.ingramcontent.com/pod-product-compliance
Lightning Source LLC
Chambersburg PA
CBHW071904070526
44583CB00016B/1831